D0205456

Celebrating
the Single Life

Celebrating
the Single Life

Keys to Successful Living on Your Own

David Yount

 PRAEGER

Westport, Connecticut
London

Library of Congress Cataloging-in-Publication Data

Yount, David.
  Celebrating the single life : keys to successful living on your own / David Yount.
      p. cm.
  Includes bibliographical references and index.
  ISBN 978–0–313–36595–9 (alk. paper)
  1. Single people—United States. 2. Single people—United States—Psychology. 3. Single people—United States—Life skills guides. I. Title.
  HQ800.4.U6Y69 2009
  646.70086'52--dc22   2008041038

British Library Cataloguing in Publication Data is available.

Library of Congress Catalog Card Number: 2008041038
ISBN: 978–0–313–36595–9

First published in 2009

Praeger Publishers, 88 Post Road West, Westport, CT 06881
An imprint of Greenwood Publishing Group, Inc.
www.praeger.com

Printed in the United States of America

The paper used in this book complies with the
Permanent Paper Standard issued by the National
Information Standards Organization (Z39.48–1984).

10 9 8 7 6 5 4 3 2 1

For Becky,
who need never walk alone

Contents

This Is What You Shall Do:
Love *the earth and sun and animals,*
despise *riches,*
Give *to everyone who asks,*
stand up *for the stupid and crazy,*
devote *your income and labor to others,*
hate *tyrants,*
argue not *concerning God,*
have patience *and indulgence towards the people,*
take off *your hat to nothing known or unknown,*
or to any man or number of men —
go freely *with powerful uneducated persons, and with the young,*
and with the mothers of families —
re-examine *all you have been told in school or church*
or in any book,
and **dismiss** *whatever insults your own soul.*
…
Your very flesh shall be a great poem,
and have the richest fluency,
not only in its words
but in the silent lines of its lips and face,
and between the lashes of your eyes,
and in every motion and joint of your body.
Walt Whitman
Preface to Leaves of Grass

Acknowledgments

No sooner had I completed a book-length manuscript extolling marriage than the U.S. Census Bureau revealed that the majority of adult Americans are no longer living in wedlock but on their own.

Of course, I would not have attempted what I called my "marriage book" had it not been for the fact that the institution of marriage has long been under siege. Being happily married myself, I devoted close to a year to determining what causes nearly half of all marriages in America to fail, and what couples might do to improve their odds of living happily ever after till death do they part.

But given the new statistic, I was forced to acknowledge that the prospect of living "happily ever after" must also be available to men and women who are single, either by choice or by circumstances such as divorce or the death of a spouse. Hence this book.

Confronted with this new statistic, I reflected on my own history of single living. I was already in my thirties when I first wed. When that marriage became history, I found myself a single parent with custody of my three little daughters.

Although I have now been married to Becky, my second wife, for close to three decades, I spent as many early years on my own as a boy and young adult. As the only child of two working parents, I learned in my early years to rely on my own resources, balancing solitude with relative freedom. Granted, the world was a less threatening place for a child then, but I was the only latch-key kid in my school and neighborhood.

If the insurance industry's predictions are correct, my wife—11 years my junior—will outlive me by many years. I'd be delighted if my better half chooses to remarry. But, more likely, she, like most widows, will have to manage the autumn of her life alone. There is nothing wiser than being prepared for life's inevitabilities. So, just as I wrote my book on marriage to honor her love, I've written this one to honor her life and help ensure her future.

This is the first of my books to rely largely on information available on the Internet. Books quickly go out of print, so I have directed readers to Web sites that offer fresh, updated resources for everything you will need to live successfully on your own at any stage in your life.

Among authors I consulted, I do wish to express my reliance on a book recommended to me by my wife, entitled *Solitude*; it is by the British psychiatrist Anthony Storrs, who documents the extraordinary accomplishments of people throughout history who have lived on their own resources. Loneliness can be a curse, to be sure, but solitude can be an extraordinary blessing. A great secret to life is to learn to cultivate and cherish your own company, becoming your own best friend.

Thanks to Praeger's Suzanne Staszak-Silva for taking an interest in this project and shepherding it into production. She also edited my previous title, *America's Spiritual Utopias: The Quest for Heaven on Earth.*

I want to express my admiration for many friends and acquaintances who successfully navigate life on their own every day, but I'm loath to name them for fear that some would protest that the single life was not of their choosing but was thrust on them, uninvited.

Above all, I am grateful to my wife and helpmate for her professional counsel and her daily companionship. I am blessed to be numbered among those men who have married above themselves.

1

Welcome to the Majority

"If you have built castles in the air . . . now put the foundations under them."

Henry David Thoreau

American society is no longer defined by marriage. Today, an increasing majority of American households are headed by single men and women. Even those Americans who do marry spend at least half of their adult lives alone. If you happen to be single—for whatever reason—it's cause for celebration and careful cultivation. Welcome to the majority.

Perhaps the traditional fixation on marriage as the key to lifelong happiness has discouraged you from pursuing the joys of successful single living. Don't fall for it. There is no single formula for life fulfillment; one size does not fit all. You must write your own script for happiness.

These days, if you are unmarried and pining for romance, you are in a small minority.[1] Only 16 percent of single Americans told the Pew Research Foundation that they were currently looking for a romantic partner. That amounts to just 7 percent of the nation's adult population. Indeed, a majority (55 percent) of singles express no active interest at all in seeking a partner. Even a greater majority of widowed, divorced, or older women are not seriously seeking romance.

Even among young adults, the zest for romance and marriage has waned. Only 22 percent of singles aged eighteen to twenty-nine admit that they are looking for life partners. Rest assured, they are not antisocial. As many as one-fourth of single young adults are in what they consider to be committed relationships, but with neither a wish nor a prospect of marriage.

This signals a tidal shift toward single living. Within recent memory, most Americans considered living alone to be transitional—awaiting the appearance of Mr. or Ms. Right to lead them to the altar, domesticity, and happily-ever-after. In the past, men and women who remained unwed were pitied by their peers and tempted to consider their state in life as selfish, unnatural, and lonely.

Welcome instead to twenty-first-century America, where men and women at any age successfully pursue their path through life relying on their own resources, with marriage merely as an option.

The new demographic is less a cause for concern than it is an invitation for singles to face the facts, take charge of their lives, and trade in dependency for autonomy. The single life can no longer be dismissed as accidental. Indeed, the vast majority of Americans, wed and unwed, need to be self-reliant.

WHAT HAPPENED TO WEDLOCK?

Why has marriage declined as society's standard? In Genesis, the Creator observed that "It is not good for man to be alone."[2] Yet, throughout history, marriage has never completely insulated couples from the human predicament. We are each born alone, die alone, and live within our own minds and souls. Today, even those Americans who elect to marry are doing so much later than ever in our nation's history.

Marriage itself is more vulnerable to divorce than ever before: newlyweds enjoy only a 50–50 chance of permanence. Those couples in second and third marriages suffer an even greater failure rate.[3]

Moreover, in the autumn of their lives, those of us who have weathered married life successfully often find ourselves alone again, having outlived our spouses. Thus the single population—young and old alike—expands. Meanwhile, the ranks of never-married men and women are growing exponentially.

Rest assured, there is every reason to celebrate the single life rather than resent it. The freedom that comes with independent living sets no limits on friendship, affection, companionship, and romance. What it does demand is that we develop the practical and emotional skills that enable us to love and be loved rather than allow ourselves to be impoverished.

WHAT HAPPENED TO ROMANCE?

Are Americans no longer romantically inclined? Don't believe it. But many younger couples (themselves the sons and daughters of divorced parents) have become wary of wedlock. Fewer of us are willing to settle for relationships that promise less than permanence and fulfillment. As a consequence, we are slower than ever to tie the knot and hastier than ever to cut it.

Our appreciation of the single life lags far behind the new reality. But there are notable exceptions. For example, one-fourth of adult New Yorkers in their twenties and thirties boast that they remain single by choice.[4] For them, living on their own in the Big Apple represents freedom and autonomy. They consider themselves winners, not compromisers. Embracing the single life, they actually socialize more than the rest of us, forging networks of friends of both sexes. Solitude does not scare them; they are not lonely.

Regrettably, many singles of both sexes cannot enjoy unalloyed freedom because they have dependents. At the same time that they must fend for themselves, they carry the added burden of supporting young children or aging parents. Responsible single parents find satisfaction in their families and friends. Surveys suggest that, as they approach their later years, fewer than one in seven aging parents will be able to count on adult children to contribute to their financial support. The average age of widows, incidentally, is just fifty-five.[5]

The single life used to be simple to grasp. Young women lived in the parental home until marriage. In Victorian times, if a suitor failed to appear before a daughter reached the age of twenty-six, she was deemed a spinster and expected to devote herself to her aging parents. By contrast, sons left the parental home as early as possible to earn enough to become eligible as husbands.

Today, single living has developed many permutations. Young women now typically leave home as soon as possible to begin careers, whereas many of their brothers continue bunking with Mom and Dad, putting their lives on hold even after they have graduated from high school or college.

VARIATIONS ON THE SINGLE LIFE

Depending on their circumstances, single men and women face different challenges. Divorced men and women of all ages are single. So, too, are widows and widowers, as well as parents without partners, whether or not their children were conceived in wedlock. Single, too, are the growing number of men and women who share life together without the mutual commitment of marriage. In truth, an unmarried couple consists of two single persons sharing a single bed.

No matter what satisfactions they seek, few unmarried American men and women consider themselves part of the "Swinging Singles" scene. Living on one's own resources is a challenge at any age and in any circumstance. To be sure, autonomous living can be an adventure, but seldom a freewheeling one. Still, it invites celebration.

It's not difficult to trace our shift from a nation of marrieds into a society of singles. Beginning in the 1960s, reliable contraception insulated sex from childbearing, as the baby boom generation took up the mantra, "If it feels good, do it." Since then, the failure rate of marriages has soared, leaving the offspring of divorced parents wary of wedlock.

One outcome is a tenfold explosion of couples living together without marriage.[6] Nowadays what was once called a "trial marriage" collapses in fewer than five years. Today, more than half of all first-time marriages are preceded by cohabitation. These informal arrangements fail twice as often as other first-time marriages.

Ironically, despite the easy availability of contraception, births to unwed mothers have soared to the point where one in every three American children enters life without the security of a married mother.[7]

Of course, economics has played a major role in converting us into a nation of singles. For example, we have long since discarded the romantic notion that two can live as cheaply as one.

Over recent decades, women have entered the workforce less for liberation than from economic necessity. Today, even when prospective spouses are both employed, men and women in their twenties and thirties continue to be saddled with huge personal debts. These include tens of thousands of dollars of unpaid college loans, which cast a pall over wedlock and then discourage couples from starting a family, even as their biological clocks keep ticking.

Whether single by choice or circumstance, we can take charge of our own lives, relishing our independence and developing a full emotional life, expanding our interests, and widening our circle of friends, all the while enriching the lives of others and making the world a better place because of us.

You can establish and maintain autonomy, paying your own way and ensuring your security, at every stage in your life. And, when you need it, you can obtain assistance without becoming permanently dependent or indebted to others.

ADVANTAGES OF BEING SINGLE

Monks and nuns choose the single life because they dedicate themselves totally to God. But they are the first to deny that celibacy is a restriction on their lives. Far from denigrating marriage, John Wesley, the great Protestant

Reformer, nevertheless praised the single life as "free from a thousand nameless domestic trials, which are found sooner or later in every family." Of the unmarried, he noted:

They are at liberty from the greatest of all entanglements, the loving one creature above all others; they have leisure to improve themselves; and, having no wife or children to provide for, may give all their worldly substance to God.[8]

Yet others choose to remain single in order to devote themselves totally to humankind. You are undoubtedly aware of doctors, scientists, political leaders, explorers, members of the military, and entrepreneurs who have chosen to remain unmarried rather than expect a spouse to be satisfied with what little of their time, attention, and even presence they can spare from their life's work.

Even if your career does not absorb the lion's share of your time, energy, and attention, your choice of the single life will allow you to pursue other interests more fully, without shortchanging the legitimate demands of a life partner.

For starters, the single life awards you more freedom and independence. You need answer to no one but yourself, avoiding reluctant compromise and emotional conflict. You will have to cook and clean for yourself, of course, but you alone will choose the menu according to your taste and you can set your own standards. You can enjoy the leisure to explore new interests that will make you a more interesting person to others and a better friend.

It is not selfish to do things for yourself that you are free to do. What is selfish is to limit someone else's freedom by tying them to you when you cannot reciprocate fully.

Happily, the single life guarantees you greater control over your time, which you may elect to spend helping others less fortunate than yourself. Alternatively, you can spend time advancing your career, going back to school, or caring for friends.

You will also maintain control of your money. Whether you are, on balance, a spender or a saver, you can make your financial decisions without depriving a life partner of his or her needs and desires.

In addition, you will be spared the annoyance of a partner's irritating habits, allowing you to concentrate on ridding yourself of your own. Nor need you nag a loved one to wash the dishes or take out the trash, because you will assume the responsibility of routine tasks yourself.

Unless you're inclined to argue aloud with yourself, yet another advantage of single living is that it will spare you emotionally from the conflicts, arguments, heartbreaks, and outbursts that accompany domestic life.

Finally, single life will allow you more time to get in touch with yourself and become a better person. Should you choose the opportunity to marry at a later stage in your life, you will be a more eligible, more wholesome, and kinder prospect.

Approach single living as an adventure in self-improvement rather than taking smug satisfaction with the person you always have been. Being on your own affords the opportunity to think and feel better about yourself, which will immediately be apparent to others and make you more attractive to them. Don't fall for the notion that you need someone else to reassure you how wonderful you are. A wise saint advised that the key to attract love is to make yourself lovable.

THE OBSTACLES YOU FACE

Despite the fact that only a minority of American households is led by married couples, you may be prone to suspecting every stranger you meet to be attached. Fight your tendency to check every attractive person to determine whether he or she is wearing a wedding band.

Suburbs and small towns attract married couples with children. If that's where you live or work, don't be surprised to discover that most of your neighbors and co-workers are wed. Many singles feel left out when their friends marry, and it's true that, once married, a couple will tend to socialize with other couples. If you are of an age to feel like a fifth wheel at social gatherings of mostly-marrieds, you will want to make an effort to seek out other singles instead. In fact, the fragile state of marriage in America today is such that couples soon find themselves socializing with singles who were formerly married. In any case, wherever you live, don't confine yourself to a home-alone ghetto. Because we live close to Washington, D.C., my wife and I are intrigued by the guest lists at White House dinners, as well as formal Congressional, embassy, press, and arts events. Significant singles in our nation's capital cultivate each other's company and pair up for these occasions. Rest assured, when Condoleezza Rice attends a White House state dinner, she goes as one-half of a couple. You will do well to cultivate a friend who enjoys your company for such occasions. In successful single living, romance is optional, but comradeship is essential.

You do want to get out and about, so make sure you have something appropriate to wear when invited. More than 20 years ago I discovered a cast-off Saks Fifth Avenue tuxedo for six dollars at a church bazaar. It's all I've ever owned for formal wear, and I seldom turn down an opportunity to dust it off and try it on.

The entertainment media is skewed toward depicting love and romance, and nearly every commercial tune is a love song. If you happen not to be in a romantic relationship, you may be tempted to believe that everyone else is in one. It's not so.

Even worse, Hollywood overwhelmingly depicts villains as single. Newspapers skew their advice columns to readers seeking romance. Every weekend, they display pages of smiling brides and handsome grooms. It can seem like a conspiracy against the unmarried. But it's just a way of selling more papers.

Married couples tend to socialize with one another because their lives are restricted to daily domesticity and children. Their conversation tends to be limited to child rearing, dealing with repairmen, and maintaining the home. Couples tend to entertain at home rather than go out. Unless you're a single parent, you won't have to worry about a baby sitter for social freedom, and you won't be confined to your own four walls.

Even if you are a single parent, you will find yourself freer than many marrieds, not least because you do not have to seek the approval of a spouse when it comes to your schedule, social life, spending, and child care. Dependency too often leads to a sense of false security. It's better to cherish the freedom that comes from depending on yourself.

MYTHS ABOUT SINGLE LIFE

Parents tend to hope that their children will be married. It's an understandable prejudice. After all, they are married. It's their experience. And, should you marry, they will soon want to know when you plan to give them grandchildren. Parents are programmed to believe that their children will never grow up until they are wed and mired in domesticity. Even if you become hugely successful as a single, they may believe that your career and other interests are trivial pursuits.

Don't try too hard to change their beliefs. After all, they only want you to be happy, and marriage and family are their formula.

But don't buy into their prejudices, because they only perpetuate myths about the single life: for example, "Single means lonely." Not at all. "Single" doesn't even mean "alone." What it does mean is that singles can more easily choose moments of solitude without taking time and attention away from the people closest to them. Singles are actually freer to choose their friends of both sexes and to expand their circle of comrades without rousing envy or jealousy among those persons who make a legitimate emotional claim on them. Marriage connotes exclusivity and possessiveness. Only the very best marriages are those in which spouses allow each other the freedom to grow and mature. A lonely single is a selfish person who is focusing on himself or herself instead of others.

Another myth is "I need someone to make me feel good about myself." A romantic relationship will never solve your problems, least of all any feelings of inadequacy. Emotional entanglements actually magnify one's shortcoming and create new problems. Putting two needy people together makes them doubly needy. Relationships are not prescriptions for curing your ills, but for sharing yourself with another person. To do that successfully, you must have self-confidence to share. Only you can make you happy, and only a "happy you" can build a successful life with another. Abraham Lincoln, reputed to be a melancholy man, nevertheless affirmed that "most people are about as happy as they make up their mind to be."[9]

"Since I can't find anyone who wants me, something must be wrong with me." The only thing that's wrong is that you dismiss the single life that you know in favor of one that you only imagine will make you happy. People focussed on searching often don't allow themselves to be found. Men or women "on the prowl" for a mate are likely to scare off any prospects. Moreover, if you sense that you are a failure for being single, your neediness and self-reproach will turn others away.

"Being single is only temporary. My real life won't begin until I'm with someone else." Treat your life as the gift that it is and make the most of it. You will never appreciate yourself until you invest in yourself and cherish your independence. You will never find real intimacy with another person until you are a complete person. To share means both giving to and receiving from another person. It is interdependence, not dependency. First invest in yourself. You will be happier, with more to give of yourself to others.

WRITING YOUR SCRIPT FOR SINGLE LIVING

Doubtless, living on your own will present specific challenges, depending on your age, health, and circumstances. So your script for celebrating single life will call for different strategies, depending on whether you are a young adult, a recently divorced person, a single parent, or someone who has been widowed.

Still, single living—by choice or necessity—requires the same core abilities—overcoming loneliness while cherishing solitude, reaching out to others, and developing a secure faith and self-respect, all the while paying your bills and maintaining your health, security, sense of humor, and your ability to love and be loved.

These abilities are not options but necessities. In twenty-first-century America, social isolation accounts for as much as a fivefold shortening of the lives of single men and women. As they age, men and women with few or no friends are more than twice as likely to develop Alzheimer's disease as those who take charge of their lives and make friends.[10]

George Bernard Shaw claimed, "The way to have a happy life is to be so busy doing what you like all the time that there is no time left to think about whether you are happy."[11]

Those are your challenges. Rest assured, you do not have to confront them alone. Others will help you. Regardless of when you begin, you can become the person that your Creator had in mind when you were given life.

There is a practical science to living successfully on our own. You can master it. Forget that old fable; you needn't be married to live happily ever after.

2

Cherish Life on Your Own

"Someday my prince will come."

Snow White

Then again, perhaps he won't. Or, over time, he may reveal that he is a frog merely masquerading as a prince, and you will toss him back in the pond. Or . . . mortality will intrude on "happily ever after," leaving contemporary Snow Whites and their Prince Charmings on their own, widows or widowers. Whatever the case, you owe it to yourself to learn to live on your own terms and with your own resources.

Probably the greatest impediment to living a happy life alone is that men and women alike yearn for love and are inclined to equate personal fulfillment with marriage. The American Association of Retired Persons (AARP) reveals that 71 percent of adults agree that "finding true love is life's top achievement." In any given month, as many as 182 million Americans seek true love via Internet dating sites.[1]

Unless we temper our romantic predilections with reality, we will spoil our chances for pursuing a happy life on our own.

When my wife's first marriage ended in divorce, she found herself suddenly single, in a strange city without a job or a place to live. Survival was the first order of business. She quickly attracted new friends, both married and single, found a place to live, and landed a job. Still smarting from the breakup of her marriage, Becky began to date aggressively.

At which point, her mother gave her a piece of advice: "When you stop looking for love, love will find you." To that wisdom Becky added St. Augustine's counsel: "In order to be loved, be lovable."[2]

I came along not long afterward and found her lovable. That was some thirty years ago. She still is lovable, and we are still married.

Most Americans marry, at least for a time. And most divorced persons harbor a wish to be married again. But the truth is that, on average, all of us, married or single, now live at least half of our adult lives on our own.

To live alone successfully you do not have to proclaim yourself a confirmed bachelor or bachelorette, rejecting any thought of marriage. But neither can you afford to be a hostage of romance. You must equip yourself to live on your own, enjoying your own company. When you achieve that, others will be attracted to you as to a magnet.

If you're still skeptical, consider this: the triumph of hope over experience.

This year, more than two million American couples will wed, wagering against dire odds that their love will last, conquering all in an adventure of lifelong romance. Each couple will spend, on average, upwards of $25,000 on the wedding ceremony, reception, and honeymoon alone. In addition, the newlyweds will purchase $4 billion worth of furniture, $3 billion of house wares, and $400 million of tableware to begin their lives together.[3]

Although weddings are big business, marriage itself has shrunk to minority status as the institution under which American households are organized and children are raised. The most common living arrangement in America today is a household of unmarried adults with no children. Nearly two-thirds of American households have no offspring at home.[4]

Desire and romance persist, but personal commitment has long since yielded to casual sex and cohabitation, especially among young adults. Today marriage is an afterthought for close to half of the couples who eventually decide to wed. Not only are couples who cohabit before marriage twice as likely to end their lives together, but the birth of a child makes their break-up an even surer thing.

Although plenty of couples remain happily married, that fact should not be allowed to persuade you that married life is the pinnacle of happiness. It may very well be, but only for those who have stuck with the marriage. A 2007 Gallup poll reports that nearly two-thirds of married men and women are happy with their personal lives, compared with only 43 percent of singles. Moreover, 60 percent of married couples in the lowest income bracket report being happier than half of singles in the highest income bracket.[5]

Don't those statistics prove that marriage makes one happy? Not at all! Any true picture would have to take into consideration the half of those marriages that end in divorce. Couples who are happy together remain married. Those who are miserable with each other return to the single life. If you persist in pining for a perfect soul mate who will make you happy, you are destined to be unhappy living on your own.

DISPENSING WITH STEREOTYPES

Rest assured, being on your own at any stage of your life does not condemn you to live like a monk or nun. Affection, friendship, love, and romance are all ingredients of a complete emotional life, and they are all available to the unmarried.

Our obstacle is that we have been conditioned to denigrate the single life. Fairy tales warn us about adults who live alone. Literature is no kinder. Think of Dickens's daft Miss Havisham in her dusty room, jilted, still wearing her tattered wedding dress. Or consider the cliché of the single woman whose only company consists of her cats. Men living alone are tarred as well, suspected of being sexual predators or serial killers.

Even when we dismiss these clichés, we suspect that anyone who lives alone for long will become eccentric. But hold on. Even so glamorous a single as the actor George Clooney kept a pet pig in his home for years as his closest companion.

I'm inclined myself to associate single living with eccentricity but to accept it as a simple expression of the freedom that people on their own enjoy. Thoreau complained that most people live lives of quiet desperation, largely because they fail to make time to get to know themselves. By thoughtless conformity, they "begin digging their graves as soon as they are born."[6] Midway through the last century, Harvard sociologist David Riesman warned that conformity had turned American society into what he termed "The Lonely Crowd."[7]

So let us celebrate eccentricity, identifying it as what it is—individuality in the adventure of enjoying one's own company. Cherish free choice. It is one of the principal advantages of living on your own, as opposed to compromising with a soul mate.

If living alone is new to you, you may feel like Thoreau venturing solo into the Massachusetts woods. But, like him, your purpose will be "to transact some private business with the fewest obstacles."[8]

That "private business" will be to get to know and like yourself and to cherish your own company.

THE PERSISTENCE OF AN ILLUSION

In her book, *The New Single Woman,* sociologist E. Kay Trimberger confronted the effects of divorce on newly single women. As she attempted a chapter entitled "Sex and the Single Woman," a friend opined, "Provocative title, but what you find will not be."

To be sure, many divorced women whom Trimberger interviewed dismissed sex as "overrated," but she discovered that those women for whom sex was a priority "almost always found it. Love, not sex, I discovered, is the elusive entity."[9]

Anyone who treats the single life as temporary, pending the appearance of a soul mate, is like a person living in a succession of unfurnished rooms. The single life is not a "meanwhile strategy," but a life worthy of permanence and integrity, one that can be filled with love and friendship.

Single men seem to accept this better than women, but they can be less adept at developing friendships that support their life alone. Still, the true test of living on one's own, for men and women alike, is not how many friends they attract but how well they get on with themselves. British social commentator India Knight writes that "being uncomfortable with your own company is a modern disease."

She acknowledges that "being single used to get an incredibly bad press—a mystery, in my view, since being on your own is infinitely preferable to being with someone ghastly . . . In the mid-1990s there was a sort of low-level panic at the idea of being left 'on the shelf.'"

Knight believes that concern to be outdated: "In past generations the energetic, eccentric maiden aunt had rather a lovely time, pottering about, driving with the roof down, reading books, having more spending money than the child-encumbered, going on holiday to exciting family-unfriendly places and looking glamorous. I don't really understand why she evolved into a sad, withered figure that inspired both pity and terror."

India Knight writes from experience. She is divorced, a single mother, and unsentimental about the single life. It is not for sissies, she affirms, and can be "incredibly hard work":

I was reminded of this the other night when a girlfriend was moaning that endless Christmas parties had taken their toll and she just wished she could have one night at home with a mug of tea, a takeaway, and something mindless on the telly. Easily arranged, I said, just don't go out. I do it all the time. But apparently not. "I have to put myself out there," she said, miserably, "otherwise who knows what—or who—I may be missing out on."[10]

Such is life striving for an illusion.

THE TRUE JOYS OF COUPLEDOM

To be sure, many live-alones are not single by choice. But the effort expended to survive in the contemporary dating scene in hopes of making a fortuitous lifelong connection is unworthy of most singles past a certain age.

The contentment that sentimental singles seek in marriage is nothing like the frantic lottery of the dating game. To be honest, what they want is freedom, along with the added comfort of a trusted companion.

Only party animals want to dance every night. The rest of us prefer to kick off our shoes at the end of the day, enjoy a home-cooked meal, watch something mindless on TV, and chat about nothing in particular with someone who is at least mildly interested.

What we want is not glamor and adventure, but comfort.

What about sex? "Lonely people can always get sex if they want it," Knight says, "but getting somebody who will happily make you a cup of tea is altogether a trickier proposition."[11] To qualify, that person does not have to be a spouse or a lover. It can be a friend, a neighbor, a workmate, or family member. If tea is less important than companionship, the answer can be a pet. Don't pity the single woman with cats or the single man with a dog. As companions, pets are vastly less demanding than people and typically quicker to accept and offer affection. No wonder there are as many pets as people in America.

THE VIRTUES OF SOLITUDE AND PRIVACY

The English psychiatrist Anthony Storrs laments that our idealization of interpersonal relationships "causes marriage, supposedly the most intimate tie, to be so unstable. If we did not look to marriage as the principal source of happiness, fewer marriages would end in tears."

He concludes that "people who have no abiding interests other than their spouses and families are as limited intellectually as those who have neither spouse nor children may be emotionally," and asks us to consider whether "what goes on in the human being when he is by himself is as important as what happens in his interactions with other people."[12]

Yet another false stereotype of living on one's own is that it is, perforce, lonely. To be sure, a strong motive for seeking companionship is to flee one's solitude. But, too often, that means escaping oneself for dependency on another person.

Being physically alone does not equate with loneliness. It's quite the opposite: when we are alone with our thoughts and daydreams, we typically resent intrusions. Equally, when we are at work or concentrating on a task, we don't wish to be disturbed. Until fairly recently, people were so crowded together physically that they felt almost claustrophobic. Single people often found themselves crowded into dormitories and boarding houses, lacking not only space but—more important—privacy. A young woman to whom I was engaged in college looked on marriage as a way to escape her crowded home. She complained that, growing up, the only place she could be alone was in the bathroom—and there was only one of those in her family's modest old house.

Ultimately, loneliness stems from a lack of self-regard. But, in the short run, it is a by-product of social isolation and a lack of personal validation by others. Not least of the damaging outcomes of divorce is to find oneself with few friends, or none. Married couples often shed their friends for each other's company. In homely terms, they place all their eggs in their partner's basket.

When a marriage breaks up, the former couple can find themselves more completely isolated than they have been since childhood. Louise Bernikow in *Alone in America* identifies loneliness as "not being known, not fitting, not being right"—even being deserted by oneself.[13] Making new friends is the first order of business. But here's a word of caution: families and spouses have an investment in keeping you just the way you are, even when you're not happy with yourself. Friends, by contrast, expect a certain reciprocity, but they encourage your autonomy.

And they do it by giving you different perspectives on yourself than you can achieve on your own. A friend with a sense of humor will appeal to your fun-loving side; a sober-sided friend can strengthen your serious side. In *Bridget Jones's Diary*, the heroine, a single woman in her thirties, worries about "dying alone and being found three weeks later eaten by dogs."[14] Bridget, of course, was obsessed with finding a soul mate. If she had invested as much attention in making friends (of both sexes), they would have kept tabs on her without invading her privacy or leaving her to the dogs.

"BUT I DIDN'T CHOOSE TO BE SINGLE."

Maybe not, but it doesn't mean that singles are victims of circumstance. If you find yourself on your own, at any stage in your life, it will be the result of choices that you have made along the way.

If you've never been married, it's because you determined that sufficiently attractive prospects weren't available. If you're divorced, it's because you determined that your marriage didn't live up to your expectations. And if you're single again because your spouse has passed away, it's because you knew from the outset that wedlock is "till death do us part"— but no longer. On average, men live shorter lives than women, yet they tend to marry women younger than themselves. On the face of it, that's an impractical decision, but it's one that couples make. The nation's nursing homes disproportionately serve women whose marriages endured, but whose older husbands passed away before them.[15]

The single life can be thrust upon us at any age, but not without our cooperation, if not actual collaboration. Still, Tennessee Williams affirmed that "the heart is a stubborn organ,"[16] but it needs exercise. Do not allow your heart to grow cold through inactivity just because you are on your own.

Although our nation was founded on our right to pursue happiness, that goal can be elusive. Dr. Martin Seligman, former president of the American Psychological Association, is the reigning expert on the subject and author of *Authentic Happiness*, which, in its first four years of publication, was translated into nearly twenty languages.

The psychologist is quick to acknowledge that happiness does not consist of mindless personal pleasure but requires community engagement, spiritual connectedness, hope, and charity. Trained as an expert on clinical depression, he decided in midcareer to explore the other side, determining what makes life worth living. Happiness, he discovered, requires attention, effort, and persistence—not just passively feeling good, but positively doing good.[17]

When a class in happiness was first announced at Harvard, it attracted the most students of any course offering on campus. In a delightful feature for *The New York Times Magazine*, author D. T. Max chronicled his experiences in happiness classes on other campuses.[18] When asked what already made them happy, his young classmates mentioned sex, drinking, entertainment, adventure, and friendship.

Given the assignment to perform acts of selfless kindness, the same students became more imaginative. One who was terrified of needles gave blood. Another donated clothes to a shelter for battered women. A third gave a waiter at a fast food restaurant a $50 tip.

Seligman is himself a student of positive psychology. When he chastised his five-year-old daughter for being whiny, she struck a deal with her Dad: if he would stop being grumpy, she would stop her whining. They both happily improved their behavior.

My own experience of happiness is that it is not a constant state. Rather, life is filled with fleeting gifts of joy that are not of our own manufacture. At best, the pursuit of happiness is an applied science, not equally available to the poor, the sick, and the handicapped—but certainly available to those who live on their own.

The Bible, incidentally, is strangely sparse in its formulas for happiness, unless we can agree with those scholars who say Jesus's Sermon on the Mount is best translated as "Happy are the poor . . . the merciful . . . the sincere . . . the peacemakers . . . and those who suffer persecution for the cause of goodness."[19]

Living on your own, you are better advised to settle for contentment and to develop a keen sense of humor instead of asking, "Am I happy yet?"

LOOK UP, BUT WATCH WHERE YOU'RE STEPPING

Self-confidence is just that—the confidence that you award yourself. Only a saint merits wholehearted self-esteem, yet saints are notoriously critical of themselves. But they are effective nonetheless because they are confident. Their self-acceptance stems wholly from their belief that their creator loves and respects them. Their self-confidence comes from working to justify that trust.

Those of us who are less than saints gain our confidence from small successes that beckon us to take further challenges. It helps, of course, to have loved ones who believe in us, but we are unlikely to believe even those closest to us unless we sense some record of success in our own efforts. School can be hard on a child who is plain, unathletic, or a slow learner. As children, we were constantly tested by our teachers, physically and mentally, against arbitrary standards and judged even more severely by our peers. Youth favors popularity as athletes, scholars, and cheerleaders. The vast majority of us, in childhood, couldn't compete successfully in those arenas. Fortunately, we aren't called on to do so as grown-ups. As adults, we find our self-confidence in different roles.

When they were young, I told my learning-disabled daughters from my first marriage that adult life would be friendlier to them than their growing-up years; that prediction proved to be true. The basis for self-confidence in adult living is choosing our challenges instead of having others impose theirs on us. Adults select the friends, loves, and interests to which they devote their lives and that bring them satisfaction. Unlike schoolchildren, adults are not expected to be good at everything, but only competent at earning a living and responsible to the persons whom they choose to involve in their lives.

Of course, we can fail at unsuitable jobs and with misplaced affections, but temporary setbacks are powerful motivation for starting afresh and moving on. Sadly, kids who fail in school are inclined to drop out, because there are no meaningful alternatives to school during the early years. But those of us who encounter failure in adulthood have alternatives—in employment, love, enjoyment, service, and every other aspect of living— that can make us successful again. If you find yourself single because of divorce or the death of a spouse, you are no less successful than you were before. But you must take initiative.

To be sure, there is a drawback to adulthood. Whereas children are constantly being evaluated, as adults we are often at a loss to know how well we are doing, both in our work and in our relationships. Expectations in our professional and personal lives are too seldom expressed by our supervisors and loved ones. To renew confidence and grow in spirit, we must insist on frequent feedback. That is especially true when you are living on your own.

I was past the age of fifty before I ever received a formal performance review in the workplace. Earlier, I was left guessing about how well my work was regarded. When I became a foundation president, I was determined to clear the air. Not only did I institute an annual review for my staff, but I insisted that my trustees give me one as well.

Periodically, in your own work and your own relationships, summon the courage to ask "How am I doing?" You will either be reassured, rechallenged, or made aware that others' expectations of you are unrealistic and need to be altered. Whatever the assessment, your spirit will not suffer, because you will be exchanging illusion for reality. The truth will make you free.

QUICK FIXES

Self-esteem is holistic. It encompasses our whole way of relating to the world—our strategies for establishing goals, our expectations, our reactions to change, and how we deal with setbacks. People with low self-esteem tune out praise and amplify anything derogatory that is said about them. They actually seek partners who think poorly of them. Because of their low opinion of themselves, battered women tend to choose the kind of men who will mistreat them. They believe, perversely, that they deserve the abuse they get.

Of course, we cannot completely eliminate the lingering effects of childhood experiences, even when we only dimly recall them. Self-esteem is affected by the ways in which the world has reacted to us in the past and continues to act toward us at present. As William Swann acknowledges, "People who feel downtrodden sometimes are downtrodden. For this reason, merely changing people's ways of feeling about themselves may create an illusion that will vanish in the harsh light of reality."[20]

Quick fixes won't work, but longer fixes can and do. It is pointless to attempt to lift yourself up by your own bootstraps when others are prepared to help you raise your spirits and help you on your adventure in living on your own. Although you're on your own, you don't have to go it alone.

In the past, people with low self-esteem and ready cash consulted expert counselors, who guided them through lengthy and often expensive therapy. Today, antidepressants offer the illusion of a cheap alternative—a quick fix to self-confidence. It is true that Prozac and similar drugs can temporarily temper sufferers' moods, but they can neither lift our spirits permanently nor strengthen our faith in ourselves.

Elizabeth Wurtzel, who took Prozac for seven years to cope with depression, credits the drug for saving her life but says it failed to change her life. In *Prozac Nation,* she revealed:

Years and years of bad habits, of being attracted to the wrong kinds of men, of responding to every bad mood with impulsive behavior (cheating on my boyfriend or being lax about my work assignments), had turned me into a person who had no idea how to function within the boundaries of a normal, nondepressive world. I needed a good therapist to help me learn to be a grown-up, to show me how to live in a world where the phone company doesn't care that you're too depressed to pay the phone bill.[21]

PREDICTABILITY

Self-confidence flies in the face of uncertainty. Every initiative that we take can end in failure rather than success, which explains why men and women with low self-esteem shy away from risk-taking altogether. But some risks actually make us stronger, even when they fail. Take the case of the ten-year-old Samuel Clemens, who as an adult would become known by his pen name, Mark Twain. In 1845, an epidemic of measles swept through his small town of Dawson's Landing, Missouri. Dozens of children perished and the rest were terrified. Rather than remain paralyzed with doubt, waiting to contract the disease, young Sam inflicted it on himself:

I made up my mind to end the suspense and settle this matter one way or the other and be done with it. Will Bowen (a playmate) was dangerously ill with the measles and I thought I would go down there and catch them . . . I slipped through the backyard and up the back way and got into the room and into the bed with Will Bowen without being observed . . . It was a good case of measles that resulted. It brought me within a shade of death's door.[22]

But the young Sam Clemens survived . . . and thrived.

As a young girl growing up in the Ohio countryside, my wife was constantly warned by her parents to avoid the poison ivy that surrounded their home. Tired of being cautious and uncertain whether she was allergic to the leaves anyway, she decided one day to roll in the stuff. Her experiment ended even more happily than Sam Clemens's—she proved to be immune to the poison. But, like him, Becky took a risk to make a discovery. Suddenly, one facet of her life became more predictable, and she became empowered to take other calculated risks.

In their quest for predictability, men and women with poor self-images take the opposite tack, embracing partners who think poorly of them, while actually shunning those who think well of them. Young Sam Clemens infected himself to make an uncertain situation more predictable and controllable; ironically, people with poor self-regard choose confirming partners for the same reason, feeling safer in abusive relationships than in uncertain ones. Choose friends who affirm and strengthen you, even when they are occasionally critical of your choices.

Fear can be good; it confronts real danger. Anxiety may be the product of depression. Uncontrolled, it can reduce you to inaction. Experiments demonstrate that people who fear thunderstorms lose that fear if they see lightning and can predict when the next thunderclap will come. Similarly, people inflicted with pain feel its agony less if they can predict when it will come. Predictability gives us a sense of control. The more we welcome risks, the more we encounter success, however modest. Life fills with novelty and more predictability. When I'm uncertain about the future, Becky typically asks, "What's the worst that can happen? And can you live with it?" Mistakes are seldom tragedies.

YOUR AUTHENTIC SELF

No one can be completely self-approving but must choose his or her own standards of self-esteem. As a child, the famed psychologist William James was berated by his father, who constantly pointed to his son's failures. As an adult, James decided to concentrate on his strengths and discount his weaknesses, "staking his salvation" on a few areas of excellence:

I am often confronted by the necessity of standing by one of my empirical selves and relinquishing the rest. Not that I would not, if I could, be both handsome and fat and well-dressed, and a great athlete, and make a million a year, be a wit, a bon-vivant, and lady-killer, as well as a philosopher, a philanthropist, statesman, warrior, and African explorer, as well a "tone-poet" and saint. But the thing is simply impossible . . . So the seeker of his truest, strongest, deepest self must review this list carefully, and pick out the one on which to stake his salvation . . . I, who for the time have staked my all on being a psychologist, am mortified if others know much more psychology than I. But I am contented to wallow in the grossest ignorance of Greek. My deficiencies there give me no sense of personal humiliation at all. Had I "pretensions" to be a linguist, it would have been just the reverse.[23]

Britain's King George VI (father of the current queen) gained the throne by default when his brother abdicated to marry the American divorcée Wallis Simpson. Afflicted all of his life with fragile health and a speech impediment, the shy monarch nevertheless led his nation through World War II, refusing to leave London during the Blitz. Despite a fear of flying, he served in the Navy Air Corps. The King knew his limitations but roused his spirit to manage them.

Anyone who aspires to be "all things to all men" is courting disillusion. But it is equally illusory to pretend *to* yourself to be something other than what you are. Nowhere is such deception more dangerous than in loving relationships. Famed feminist Gloria Steinem confessed that she was so determined to get a man to fall in love with her that she created a false self—changing herself into the woman that he wanted her to be. She was already well aware of the fearfulness of change:

Change, no matter how much for the better, still feels cold and lonely at first—as if we were out there on the edge of the universe with wind whistling past our ears—because it doesn't feel like home. Old patterns, no matter how negative and painful they may be, have an incredible magnetic power—because they do feel like home.[24]

Knowing change to be harrowing, Steinem nevertheless adopted a false identity to please her lover, in the process forfeiting her personal values, diminishing herself rather than lose the man she loved. But she saw clearly: "having got this man to fall in love with an unauthentic me, I had to keep on not being myself." To her credit, and on behalf of her self-confidence, Steinem at length gave up the man and reaffirmed her original self.[25]

Academy Award-winning actress Jane Fonda revealed in her memoirs that, from childhood and through her marriages, she was the victim of parents' and husbands' overblown expectations of her. Only after many years living on others' agendas did she find and assert her real self through living on her own.[26]

In order to cherish living on your own, you don't want to become an altogether different person—just a more effective, self-confident one.

RESOURCES

Getting Started

Social scientist Stephen M. Johnson argues that anyone who aspires to live the good life alone needs first to settle on a job description and then make an inventory of the skills needed to be autonomous. On a separate sheet of paper, rate your current ability to meet present needs as Excellent, Good, Adequate, Fair, or Poor:

Cooking
Housekeeping

Transportation

Money management

Clothing management

Tolerating or enjoying being alone

Enjoying solitary activities, interests, hobbies

Pursuing a satisfying career

Caring for children (if applicable)

Making and cultivating same-sex friends

Making and cultivating other-sex friends

Being with or communicating with friends regularly

Entertaining friends at home

Initiating outside activities with friends

Ease in receiving and reciprocating affection

Ease in rejecting unwanted sexual advances

Maintaining a positive mood

Assuming that you acknowledge any of your skills in these areas to be only Fair or Poor, ask yourself the following questions: "How important is that skill to me?" "How easy would it be for me to develop it?"

For example, you don't have to be a gourmet cook to eat well, but eating well is important for your overall well-being. It's actually easy to learn to cook, but you need to make it a priority in life on your own. Alternately, keeping your home or apartment neat and clean may not be a high personal priority, but you can acknowledge that it wouldn't take an immense effort to be an adequate housekeeper.

Don't be surprised about the need to manage affection and reject unwanted advances. You may be single, but you're not a hermit. Your emotional life is important to your satisfaction and your autonomy.

If you feel yourself to be seriously handicapped in summoning the confidence to live on your own, you may want to seek counseling. Clergy are among the most sensible counselors available, and they charge nothing for their services. You do not have to be a member of a congregation (or even a believer) to ask for an interview with a member of the clergy. If need be, he or she will refer you to a low-cost, full-time professional counselor. Should you be unacquainted with the churches in your community, phone the largest one or the local ministerial association listed in your White Pages to get a referral.

Short of counseling, here are a few books that may be of help in building the foundations for your self-confidence:

William B. Swann, Jr., *Self-Traps: The Elusive Quest for High Esteem* (New York: W. H. Freeman & Co., 1996).

Anthony Storr, *The Integrity of the Personality* (New York: Ballantine, 1992).

Gloria Steinem, *Revolution From Within: A Book of Self-Esteem* (Boston: Little, Brown, 1992).

Charles J. Givens, *SuperSelf: Doubling Your Personal Effectiveness* (New York: Simon & Schuster, 1993).

Peter McWilliams, *Love 101: To Love Oneself Is the Beginning of a Lifelong Romance* (Los Angeles: Prelude Press, 1997).

Thomas R. Blakeslee, *Beyond the Conscious Mind* (New York: Plenum, 1996).

Judy Ford, *Single: The Art of Being Satisfied, Fulfilled, and Independent* (New York: Reed Paperback, 2004).

Here's a CD course that comes highly recommended: Dr. Michael S. Broder, *The Single Life: How to Make It Work for You With or Without a Relationship* (Media Psychology Associates, 2006).

There is strength and wisdom in numbers. Singles are increasingly helping one another to succeed, notably through the following Web sites:

www.SingleEdition.com caters especially to thirty-two- to forty-five-year-olds and includes legal, financial, and lifestyle advice.

www.quirkyalone.net offers links to other helpful sites.

www.singleshelp.org offers a free short course in successful single living plus personal counseling.

www.unmarried.org is designed to help you establish control of your life.

www.Christianity.com is an evangelical site. Consult its Single Issues Forum.

www.TheSinglesCafe offers a comprehensive collection of articles for singles.

3

Care for Yourself

"We have all known the long loneliness, and we have learned that the only solution is love."

Dorothy Day (*The Long Loneliness*)

The long-running television series, *Sex and the City*, portrayed the adventures of four single women who were fast approaching their "use by" dates. Although each lived alone in anonymous New York City, not one of them confessed to feeling lonely despite their passionate pursuit of life partners.

Unlike most men or women in real life who live alone, Carrie, Charlotte, Miranda, and Samantha had every reason not to be lonely. Each had an engaging career, money to spend, a high sense of fashion, physical attractiveness, a full social life, and no dependents. Best of all, they had each other—dependable, straightforward friends.

Scriptwriters for the series carefully crafted the quartet's friendship to benefit each member. Notably, the women didn't compete with each other at work or for the same men. They were instantly available to each other and always spoke the truth. Each had a distinctly different personality, allowing her to offer her particular character strengths to the friendship and, at the same time opening her weaknesses to her friends' better wisdom. Of course, each was wiser about her friends than about herself, but that is true of all of us. It's one good reason to have good friends.

Sex and the City was less a fantasy about the pursuit of romance than it was about the satisfaction of living on one's own. But in real life (your life) those satisfactions can occasionally appear to be fleeting and fragile, whereas loneliness seems to be permanent.

What's worse, unlike Carrie and her friends, you may be not be totally free, but financially and personally responsible for parents or children. Or you may lack a challenging career, the reassurance of enough money to spend, a satisfying social life, a circle of dependable friends, perfect health, or physical attractiveness. Say hello to real life.

It's the rare person living alone who does not occasionally dread loneliness. This book is not intended for Carrie and friends in fantasy New York, but for singles in real life. The first secret of successful single living is caring for yourself. To do that, you first have to confront and conquer the moody blues.

THE LONELINESS BUSINESS

More than twenty years ago, writer Louise Bernikow anticipated twenty-first-century America, in which a majority of men and women live on their own. She set out on a transcontinental fact-finding mission to discover how single men and women of all ages and conditions actually disarm loneliness and find companionship. Her findings, contained in her classic book, *Alone in America*, portray the disconnectedness and feeling of emptiness that mark too many of us in our solitary society.

Bernikow acknowledges starting her journey with a prejudice—that loneliness belongs to life's losers—but quickly corrected herself. The dictionary definition of loneliness is a longing for companionship, but it neglects to suggest how much "society" satisfies that longing. Bernikow acknowledged that "alone" and "lonely" were not the same—that many people were perfectly happy to spend time alone or live alone. Moreover, "solitude" is the happy flip side of being on one's own. It's the satisfaction of having privacy, freedom, and comfort in one's own skin and even of cultivating oneself as one's own best friend.

She quickly discovered that one person's loneliness is not another's. "Some," she says, "are lonely eating alone, reminded of something that isn't there, a family, an idea of family. Some are perfectly happy eating alone but can't go to movies by themselves."

Big cities make some people lonely; others feel empty and alone in nature, missing the human presence of city life. Lonely means "nobody cares about me" often enough, a lack of relatedness to other people, feeling shut out. It sometimes means wanting a mate, or it means being married and having no friends. Many people use the word to describe a feeling of being adrift in the universe, atomized, living in a world that comprises only the self.[1] Whatever the occasion, loneliness is something that people dread—the principal impediment to pursuing a satisfying single life.

Over time, Bernikow discovered that, for many people, loneliness was the sense of time weighing on their hands, "not knowing what to do with yourself." Chronically lonely people turn to the telephone, the television, and the Internet to achieve the illusion of companionship. Unfortunately, they are only fooling themselves. Advertisers and the media abet the illusion.

For example, when I was growing up, no one I knew made a long-distance telephone call, except to announce a birth or death in the family. Whereas today we are urged to "reach out and touch someone" by phone, or we nurture the illusion that the cast members of "Friends" are our own personal friends. Beer and liquor commercials on television never depict solitary drinkers. Instead, drinking is promoted as a social pastime with happy companions.

At length, Bernikow concluded that most lonely singles are men and women who have failed to come to grips with changes in their lives. Here are some examples: An adolescent in transit from the dependency of childhood to the autonomy of adult life has not yet assimilated the change from one condition to another. A divorced person has not yet found a way of being in the world that was not as "wife" or "husband" to someone. A man who wants to fall in love with a woman who will be there at the end of the day and a woman who needs a man who makes more money than she does and will be counted on to care for, protect, and define her have not yet come to terms with the different way that we see these things now. A retired person or a widow living far from the old family circle has not found a way to adapt to those circumstances.[2]

CAN I PUT YOU ON HOLD?

Loneliness can be caused by nostalgia for something that we haven't actually lost because we never had it, such as the fanciful memory of a golden age that never was. Often it is a question of selective memory. If you are divorced, you may linger over the good times in your marriage although they were few. If you are a young adult on your own, your loneliness may take the form of yearning for your family home when, in fact, you felt confined and dependent as an adolescent.

In otherwise comfortable retirement, loneliness can suggest that we were formerly happy throughout our work lives. In every case, loneliness fancies that times were better in the past, or that we might now be contenders for happiness if fate had only favored us with better looks, education, health, or friends.

Loneliness, in brief, is the condition of standing still—of reluctance to moving on in order to make the very best of our current conditions and prospects. Loneliness often consists of waiting for something better to come along, without bothering to define that something or making the effort to grasp it.

Although loneliness can be discouraging, it is not a manifestation of clinical depression, to be relieved by medication or psychotherapy. As long as we are unreconciled to being on our own, we are inclined to believe that our lives are "on hold," waiting for something better to come along. That kind of loneliness can become an addiction equally as potent as drugs or alcohol.

Men and women feel loneliness differently. Once upon a time, "personal" ads appeared, principally in sex magazines, whose subscribers sought partners for pleasure, typically on a hit-and-run basis. But "women seeking men" and "men seeking women" ads have long since gone mainstream—in magazines, newspapers, and on the Internet. As Louise Berkinow learned, "Everyone who wants to 'meet someone' has a purpose: to close the door on being single . . . The pitch has changed. Now finding a partner and escaping singlehood is the promise of the loneliness business."[3]

THE ADVANTAGES OF SOLITARY LIVING

As my parents' only child, I made an early acquaintance with solitude. Both of them worked outside the home, so I was on my own daily from the age of seven or eight. But I spent a lot of time in the homes of school friends, all of whom had brothers and sisters. I found their sibling rivalry exotic, and I marveled at the competitive chaos in their homes. My friends, in turn, envied me for being unobliged to compete with siblings.

Over time, I found being the constant focus of my parents' attention to be oppressive and delighted in the opportunity to go away to college. My college years were close to utopian. I continued to have the solitary freedom that I had always enjoyed, but now I joined a fraternity (gaining my first brothers) and made friends of both sexes who pursued similar interests and freely shared their enthusiasms. Half a century after graduation, my classmates are still close because of the life that we shared for just four years.

To be sure, going off to college for four or more years has become hideously expensive. Yet it offers perhaps the best introduction to a life that is at once long on solitude and comfortably social. Moreover, the college years also afford the opportunity to act out the frustrations and kinks of adolescence and then to graduate into adulthood.

Actress Anne Hathaway ("The Princess Diaries"), determined not to become an undereducated Hollywood brat, settled far from the movie capital, to pursue studies at New York University between films. Freely confessing to having been a difficult child in her teens, she credits her campus experience with affording her a benign opportunity to straighten out the kinks in her character—out of the public eye. Hathaway pities the young Hollywood celebrities whose antics lead them to drugs and alcoholism—all because they lack the opportunity to expand their minds and cultivate smart and noncompetitive friends. "We've all done things we shouldn't," she admits, "it's just that I did stuff at college, when nobody knew about it, so I'm not a saint . . . I wasted time doing self-destructive things, but it didn't work. I found you can only dance on so many table tops. I got that out of my system, and now I'm healthy and I'm grounded."[4]

It's a stretch to treat a movie star as a model for every single, but Hathaway has been wise to invest not only in a glamorous career but in expanding her mind and curiosity and in assembling a wide circle of friends with whom she can share her enthusiasms. Those are the basic ingredients of a satisfying single life.

AUTONOMOUS ADULTHOOD

In *First Person Singular: Living the Good Life Alone*, Stephen M. Johnson, a clinical psychologist, urges singles to give themselves a job description. "I am convinced," he says, "that one of the primary reasons people have such difficulty in living single is that they are simply unaware of what they need to do in order to live a reasonably fulfilling life alone."[5]

Some thirty years ago, author Erica Jong complained that it was "heresy in America to embrace any way of life except as one half of a couple." Well, times have changed, and that heresy has become the new orthodoxy. Although most adult Americans today are unmarried, few have bothered to reflect on what single life entails.

Dr. Johnson originally came up with the concept of "autonomous adulthood" to assist men and women who were going through separation and divorce to land on their feet. But it soon became apparent to him that autonomy applies to all adults "irrespective of their marital or relationship status."[6]

If you are single now but hope for a life companion someday, you want to build on the satisfaction that you already enjoy on your own. The false alternative is to believe that a future mate will be a miracle worker who will make you happy. The truth is this: if you feel inadequate on your own, you can never forge an equal partnership with another person; you will be dependent on him or her. Modern marriage, after all, is an equal partnership; you have to bring your autonomous individuality to it.

Here is Johnson's challenge to singles of all ages and both genders:

What do you think could happen if you could commit yourself to living well alone as completely as you might to a really good career, relationship, marriage, or family? What if you committed yourself to learning autonomy skills with the same enthusiasm you might muster to learning a new sport? What if you spent as much energy in developing yourself as a functioning single adult as you have spent on your education, career, or family? What if you viewed single life as an exciting challenge in which much could be learned rather than as a temporary discomfort to be endured?[7]

SOLITUDE IS NOT LONELY

Human culture has had precious little experience of the single life. From ancient times people have huddled together for mutual protection. In dangerous times, protection trumps privacy, and tribal living subordinates the individual to the group. It is only in recent centuries that men and woman have separated their individuality from the communities to which they belong.

In the early centuries of Christianity, individual believers fled from pagan civilization to become solitaries, but, when the hermits became eccentric, they were lured back into monasteries to enjoy the benefits of communal life.

Self-awareness itself is a product of modern times. The communes of the 1960s represented a reversion to tribal living, typically suppressing their members' individuality and sometimes resulting in blind obedience to cult leaders.

It is worthy of note that our heroes and heroines have always been private persons—self-aware and secure in their solitude. If the prospect of living alone strikes us as scary, it is because we are not nearly as self-sufficient and self-aware as we think we are. Even rebels from conventional society eventually become uncomfortable in their own skins, so they seek the company of fellow eccentrics.

Samuel Johnson in the eighteenth century both praised and chided solitary individuals. "The solitary mortal," he said, "is certainly luxurious, probably superstitious, and possibly mad."[8]

But that was at a time when single living was the exception. Today, men and women living on their own are the rule. Perhaps the principal contribution of marriage and family life is that it civilizes its members. Spouses and parents keep us from trampling on others, while smoothing the rough edges of our character and ensuring that we act responsibly.

Let us look instead to life's heroes and heroines as models for single living. They cherish solitude and do not find it lonely—but rather an opportunity for personal growth, self-awareness, and resolution. Before embarking on his public life, Jesus of Nazareth went into the desert alone for forty days and nights. The Gospel acknowledges that he ended that ordeal hungry, but not lonely. Abraham, the Buddha, and Mohammed all sought solitude and did not find it lonely. St. Paul and Nelson Mandela used their prison solitude to seek and find their best selves, whereas Adolf Hitler used his solitary incarceration to create *Mein Kampf*, a blueprint for evil.

Samuel Johnson was correct in judging solitude to be "luxurious." It is a luxury for single persons to have the time and occasion to learn about themselves and their satisfactions. Of course, solitude suits some people more than others. Some of us are ambivalent about privacy, preferring the distraction of company. But British psychiatrist Anthony Storr insists that solitude is essential for serious thinking and self-satisfaction. In his book, *Solitude: A Return to the Self*, Storr profiles an array of men and women of great accomplishment for whom solitary life proved to be the key that unlocked their genius.

My wife once had the opportunity to spend an evening with the actress Helen Hayes, who was an intimate friend of the reclusive Greta Garbo. Garbo is best remembered for her line, "I want to be alone." "Did Garbo really cherish solitude?" my wife inquired. Oh yes, despite many friends, Greta despised celebrity and thoroughly enjoyed her own company. In later life, Helen Hayes revealed that she and Lillian Gish kept Garbo company. What subject dominated the chatter of that celebrated trio of singles? *Men!*

Henry David Thoreau is the renowned American exponent of the solitary life, and his experiment of living alone at Walden Pond is a classic example of the satisfactions that one can find in solitude. When, at length, the hermit of Walden returned to society, he had learned "that if one advances confidently in the direction of his dreams and endeavors to live the life which he has imagined, he will meet with a success unexpected in common hours."[9]

"Love your life," Thoreau urges us. "Meet it and live it. If I were confined to a corner of a garret all my days, like a spider, the world would be just as large to me while I had my thoughts about me." Solitude allowed Thoreau the freedom to make no compromises. "Remember," he advised, "only that day dawns to which we are awake. There is more day to dawn. The sun is but a morning star."[10]

THE CHALLENGE OF SOLITARY LIVING

So merely being alone doesn't produce loneliness. We all crave solitude, if for no better reason than that we need privacy. It's only when time hangs on their hands that singles are tempted to feel sorry for themselves.

Here's proof: my home is only a few minutes from Interstate 95, the nation's principal East Coast highway connecting Maine with Florida. In my little part of Northern Virginia, I-95 is not principally used by interstate travelers, but by local commuters driving daily to and from their jobs in Washington, D.C. They move at a snail's pace, while express lanes that are open to cars with three or more occupants are practically empty.

Commuters put up with traffic congestion because they insist on driving alone. Married or single, they opt for solitude over company. Most motorists, I assume, are not thinking deep thoughts as they creep along, but just listening to the radio or a CD. Some boast that they use their time alone to listen to audio books. But all of them opt for solitude over company, even when they merely fill it with distractions.

It's how well people employ their time alone that determines how successful and satisfying single life can be. That takes effort to indulge enthusiasms, appreciate legitimate pleasures, and cultivate good friends. It means not only caring for oneself but taking care of yourself.

Barbara Holland reveals the bleak alternative in her book *One's Company: Reflections on Living Alone:*

Small but ominous cracks and leaks in the good life; evenings in June when the late sun slants into the apartment and the silence ticks like a bomb; Saturdays in October when the wind creaks down the street and the light chills and sharpens and the skin prickles relentlessly.[11]

Divorced and living alone in the Blue Ridge Mountains of Virginia, Holland reflects on those men and women who are too old or too shy or too poor to consider themselves "singles":

. . . or they were recently members of families and are still unadjusted and confused, or they live in the wrong sort of place. They buy a half-loaf of bread and a can of tuna and let themselves into their apartments at the end of the day calling wistfully for the cat, check the unblinking light on the answering machine, and sit down to read through the junk mail, absorbing messages about carpet sales and grocery coupons sent in from the great busy world.[12]

PICK YOURSELF UP, BRUSH YOURSELF OFF, AND START ALL OVER AGAIN

It's no wonder that the single life suffers such a rotten reputation when it can be depicted as a kind of endless desert of the soul—a relentless loneliness. Lamentably, single life inherits its bad reputation from the very people who write and talk about it. The typical printed guide to living alone is written by a divorced or widowed woman for whom the single life is an unwelcome condition to be coped with, not embraced—an unwelcome setback thrust upon her.

Most books about the single life are, in reality, guides for surviving divorce. They sustain the notion that married life is the ideal standard for living and that single life only an aberration. In truth, the loneliness that is blamed on living alone is shared by married persons as well. Loneliness is simply part of the human condition. Marriage is not its remedy. Couples too often part because they blame their spouse for failing to cure them of their loneliness, only to find themselves feeling worthless in the absence of a life partner.

Popular advice columnists routinely counsel unhappy spouses to communicate more openly with each other, and they are right. But verbal and physical intimacy alone cannot cure us of our common human condition. As psychologist Stephen Johnson notes of every individual:

No one can experience our problems, our pain, our life as we experience them. In the final analysis all of us are alone. And yet we are dependent on other people for many things (though not as dependent as we sometimes feel) . . . You can use the pain of loneliness to discover more about yourself and life, and you can learn how to make voluntary solitude more valuable and fun.[13]

Frankly, one significant advantage in being unmarried is that you don't have a partner telling you who you are and what you owe your spouse to make him or her happy. But you do have to define yourself, your pleasures, values, and aspirations if you are to convert loneliness into satisfying solitude. Dr. Johnson suggests examining yourself to determine which of these conditions may apply to you:

1. Other people are really important to you, but you haven't taken adequate time for them.
2. Other people, while important to you, aren't everything for you, and some unwanted time alone is the price you have to pay for devoting yourself to other things.

3. You have been (a) too proud, (b) too lazy, or (c) too fearful to put yourself into situations where you can meet others.

4. Your relationships with others are superficial and leave your need for intimacy unfulfilled.

5. Because of painful relationships in the past, you have been avoiding people who could be important to you now.

6. You are allowing your lack of a partner to restrict your contact with important friends who are paired.

7. You are doing some things that drive people from you, such as (a) complaining too much, (b) depreciating yourself excessively, (c) being too aggressive, or (d) withholding yourself.

8. You are particular about friends and prefer being alone to being with people who do not meet your needs.

9. You have very few meaningful activities to engage in when alone.

10. You have for a long time lived with others and, as a result, being alone is strange and fear-provoking.

11. You have just gone through some transition in your life and need time to accumulate new friends.

12. You don't know how to have fun by yourself—you never had to learn; no one ever taught you.

13. Your limited interests make you boring to others and to yourself.

MYTHS ABOUT DEALING WITH LONELINESS

Men and women who find themselves single again after divorce are not just demoralized, but diminished. They often discover that married life itself deprived them of skills that they once possessed and that they must regain in order to resume a satisfying single life.

Typically, newlywed couples gradually give up the friends and interests that sustained them in single life, so they find themselves more alone than ever after marital breakup. It takes a concerted effort to catch up to where they were socially before they married. Moreover, men and women whose last experience of single living was in their carefree twenties quickly learn that they cannot duplicate that experience now that they are in their forties or fifties. They must start all over again with a new model of successful single life.

Here are a few of the necessities that every single must provide for: (1) somebody nearby whom you can call in distress; (2) a few people you can drop in on for company with little advance warning; (3) some friends you can join for recreation; and (4) someone who can lend you money in a pinch or can otherwise assist you in need. In short, you need to have a circle of friends. Unfortunately, according to Dr. Johnson, many singles unnecessarily restrict their friendships because they subscribe to the following myths:

1. Lovers are better than friends.
   When there's a chance to go on a date, some singles quickly cancel plans that they have already made with close friends. To do so is to choose a stranger over a friend, denigrating friendships.

2. Friendships needn't be pursued, just allowed to happen.
   It is perverse to pursue partners of the opposite sex actively without expending equal effort in making same-sex friends.

3. Singles should confine their friendships to other singles.
   My wife's best friend for decades has been a never-married woman whom she met in graduate school. Despite the differences in their domestic lives, they have a vast array of common interests and values.

4. Close friends must be of the same sex.
   If you believe this, you have written off half the human race as potential friends. As more and more young singles have the experience of living in coed college dormitories and in group houses after they graduate, they quickly learn that the opposite sex is not just for romance, but for genuine, undemanding friendship.

5. Best friends are the only real friends.
   We choose friends not because they share all of our interests and enthusiasms, but because they are comfortable to be with and reliable in a pinch. The friend with whom you choose to go shopping or to a ball game may not be the one to share books and music with—or even confidences. All friends are mutual givers, but each friend has something special to give.

6. Friends will always be there.
   Your friends have problems and needs of their own. Friends who cling too closely to each other typically have too few friends. Friendship is not dependency, but liberation. Cultivating friends allows you to share yourself and to get outside of yourself.[14]

MAKING FRIENDS

The antidote to loneliness is friendship. Making friends takes effort. You can't simply rest with responding to others' initiatives; you must take the initiative yourself. Otherwise, the friends you attract will appeal to only a few of your interests. What you want is to find companions who actually expand your interests and add some adventure to your life. If your only friends are your coworkers, they may be adequate for having a drink after work or for shopping during your lunch break. But there's more to your life than partying and shopping.

What you must do is to conduct an honest assessment of your interests and then join groups or share activities with others who have the same interests. This is such obvious advice that I hesitate to offer it. But I do, because these potential friends won't just appear spontaneously in your life. You must place yourself where they are.

If you are religious, don't keep your spirituality to yourself. Join a church that offers challenging programs for members of all ages, married and single. If you like music, don't sit at home alone listening to your CDs. Go to concerts. If you like to dance, get out and take dance lessons. Rest assured, you will not want for partners. If you like books, don't just read at home. Join a reading group that discusses the kinds of books that you like to read. If you're into sports, don't just sit in front of your television. Join a team, or find a group of compatible men or women who like to watch games together.

In an earlier book, I even suggested becoming a volunteer coach or fireman or woman. Don't just rely on your current enthusiasms. Look for adventures that open new worlds to you.

In reaching out, you're not looking for a "best" friend. Rather, you are seeking out people with similar interests who might be candidates for varying degrees of companionship. Attempting to make friends by spending weekends at singles bars with drinking buddies may net you attention, but not the kind that you need or want.

There are singles who swear by the Internet as a source of friends, but more often go online trawling for romance. In either case, cyber-friend-making is abstract, lacking real human contact. One of my daughters, still single in her thirties, works with children, lacking daily contact with potential adult friends. She has gone to the Internet in search of local women her age "to hang out with." She acknowledges that her quest is not specific enough and that she should specify her interests and join groups when looking for a social life.

Here's fair warning: people who use the Internet to make connections often misrepresent themselves, which is another way of saying that they are liars. That's not how to start a friendship. Administrators of two of the most popular Web sites were shocked to learn in 2007 that close to a third of members purporting to be single were actually married, and tens of thousands were actually registered sex offenders.[15]

Strangers can be dangerous. That's why you need to take the initiative to join groups whose members and interests are already known to one another. Don't be lazy. Meet people face-to-face, not just in cyberspace. Being single, you enjoy the advantage of the time to expand your horizons.

RESOURCES

Romance and Friendship

Dating services are typically commercial and local. Check your Yellow Pages and ask for references. In all larger communities, there are also non-profit networks, often sponsored by church groups. Usually you do not have to be a church member to join most "singles" or "young professionals" groups. Look for large churches in neighborhoods where singles live. There's no guarantee that you will find love, but you will make friends and find support. If you are divorced or a single parent, call your local chapter of Parents Without Partners.

The Internet abounds in services that promise to connect you with a compatible partner. The best ones require you to complete a personality profile and provide some credentials before accepting your application. EHarmony.com and MySpace.com offer the advantage of many members to connect with. Remember that Web sites provide only impersonal introductions (never a chaperone), so be careful connecting with strangers. If you consider yourself especially comely and insist on a mate with looks to match yours, try BeautifulPeople.net, an international dating service. But be prepared to be rejected altogether from consideration if existing members of the opposite sex turn you down on the basis of the photo you submit.

Fortunately, there are free services that rate these organizations, as well as provide direct links to them. The rating services not only offer membership details but include endorsements, as well as warnings from singles who have used them. Try date.com to get started. Incidentally, you don't have to own your own computer and possess Internet access in order to avail yourself of these opportunities to expand your social world. Just use your public library. Ask the reference librarian for help in getting started.

4

Reach Out to Others

At the moment, single men and women in Germany enjoy an advantage over their American counterparts in connecting with others. They can actually find love and friendship at their neighborhood Wal-Mart. Every Friday evening from 6 to 8, at all 91 German Wal-Marts, is Singles Night, where the price of admission is simply to show up and accept a big bright red bow to display on your shopping cart or basket.

It's up to single shoppers to strike up conversations on their own, but Wal-Mart managers assist by designating "flirting points" around the stores that stock "romantic" merchandise such as chocolates, wine, and cheese. The Singles Night concept is already being tested on singles in Puerto Rico, South Korea, and Britain, and being considered by managers in the United States.

Some of the German Wal-Mart stores actually provide bulletin boards and "mail boxes" for singles. Anyone reaching out for friends or mates can post his or her picture on the board at any time and receive responses from prospects in a private letter box. As you might imagine, the scheme has attracted single men and women of all ages who would hesitate to search for a friend or mate on the Internet or via a dating service. When a seventy-four-year-old German man confessed that he was attracted by the photo of a woman his exact age, Wal-Mart personnel played Cupid by sprucing him up and having the store's portrait photographer take his picture for her to see on the bulletin board. As a result, the septuagenarians are now dating. And, yes, some couples who first met at Wal-Mart have married. Many more have found friends of both sexes.

In midtown Manhattan, it's not Wal-Mart that attracts singles in search of companionship. Rather, it's the New York Public Library, which offers challenging lecture series. It may sound stuffy, but it appeals to urban singles who are interested in learning and in sharing their thoughts and interests. Within just two years, the average age of lecture-goers dropped from sixty-eight to forty-one, reflecting the interest of singles of all ages. Such opportunities to meet other minds and share interests are also offered at New York's Asia Society, Museum of Modern Art, and the Housing Works Used Book Café in Soho. In Washington, D.C., the Smithsonian's Hirshhorn Museum offers a series that attracted 1,700 men and women the first night.

CONNECTING

All humans look for love and cherish friendships. Unfortunately, many singles look in the wrong places because they are unaware of their options or their own minds. Sex can be purchased, but affection is priceless. Love is free, but it must be reciprocal, and it comes without a lifetime guarantee. Nor is romance the only connection worth our quest. Whatever their age, men and women need friendship, too, and affection, not just exclusive and passionate relationships.

The decline of marriage as an American institution is largely because singles are increasingly seeking "the One" who alone can make them whole and happy for a lifetime. In searching for "the One," singles are acting as consumers rather than as potential friends, lovers, and fellow-travelers. If there were truly just one person in the whole wide world to suit you, your chances for encountering him or her would be infinitesimal.

Even if you believe that marriages are made in heaven, you have to meet someone on Earth, which is a pretty big place. Only Adam and Eve had no choice in the matter. It's more likely that there are potentially tens of thousands of potential mates who could offer you a satisfying alternative to the single life.

Of course, there are matchmakers who are willing (typically for a fee) to help you find love and friendship. *The Washington Post* matches men and women in their twenties and thirties through its "Date Lab," charging no fee—but insisting on publishing the story of how the couple's first encounter went. When thirty-four-year-old Stacia Zeimet met blind date Russell Holt, thirty-eight, at a restaurant, he didn't rise to greet her. The *Post* purposely chose not to inform the pretty teacher that Russell was wheelchair-bound. The date went well enough, principally because Stacia instantly overcame her first thought, "Oh, I wasn't expecting this!" But afterward, Stacia spent days being angry at the *Post's* matchmakers. "I felt like I was set up," she says. "I'd look like a jerk, and he'd just be 'the handicapped guy.' I also didn't think it was fair to him—what if I had turned out to be a mean, tactless person?"[1]

SOUL MATES, CASUAL SEX, AND SECOND CHANCES

Even those singles who don't insist on finding "the One" often refer to their quest for intimacy as the search for a "soul mate" (as opposed to a mere "body mate"). Doubtless, dating services place a priority on physical attractiveness and on the professional status of their subscribers, but it is possible to dig deeper.

Once upon a time, couples discovered each other in church. The Internet attempts to offer a solid spiritual alternative for a soul as well as a body and for financial security. The interfaith Beliefnet.com's Soul mate Web site joined with Yahoo! Personals in late 2006 to create a pool of 14 million singles who were willing to match their spiritual chemistry with one another.

More than 20,000 young Christian women find inspiration for connecting at authenticgirl.com, which affirms traditional virtues of femininity, purity, and romance. Leslie Ludy, twenty-eight, is author of *Authentic Beauty*, which reassures young singles that being realistic doesn't require lowering standards in the search for friends and mates.

If you are formerly married and newly single, your reconnecting may not lead to a new spouse at all, but to new friends, even some of other species. As I write, Nessie, my Scottish terrier, snuggles under my feet, while cats Ginger and Rufus encourage me from a safer distance. Who knows?—perhaps affection will arrive in your life on four paws, or even on the wing. Animals are a joy, a comfort, and only a modest responsibility. As a girl, my wife had a pet lamb, whereas my mother's final years were brightened by a canary's song. Mom named the bird "Happy" because it made her so.

Typically, men and women who find themselves single again after divorce approach new relationships more sensibly, knowing that they got off on the wrong foot the first time around.

Today, half of American high school students have already engaged in sexual intercourse, and one in six teenage boys and girls has had four or more sexual partners. Sex is no longer the mystery it was when I was growing up. But oddly, the casualness of passion among contemporary young people has made them wary of one another. Familiarity has not made their hearts grow fonder. Columnist Carolyn Hax, who regularly advises the "under 30 crowd" about relationships for *The Washington Post*, writes:

These modern times are utterly devoid of dating rules and methods, courtesy of the free-love freaks of a certain generation that I won't name except to say that it rhymes with "maybe tumors." Now we're supposedly unfettered by stiff social rituals, and therefore free to mix and match with people based purely on character and chemistry. Thanks guys! Except you forgot those rituals helped people meet in the first place, which strikes me as a rather crucial step, and they came in very handy when it was time to send men home to their own beds.[2]

A former colleague of my wife's, Dr. Arthur Levine, the president of Columbia University Teachers College, surveyed 9,100 students, including focus groups on thirty campuses across the nation. He discovered that students prefer casual sexual liaisons to emotional intimacy and commitment. "When students talked about relationships, the majority said they'd never seen a successful adult relationship in their lives," the study revealed. "They're scared of relationships, of deep involvement, and that doesn't happen. Sex does happen. One way you overcome the fear of a relationship is you get loaded first, and after getting loaded you go back to somebody's room and do it."[3] Needless to say, this is not a formula for a satisfying single life.

MATCHMAKERS

So here we are in the twenty-first century trying to retrieve something that used to come without thinking. Consider this ad from *The Washington Post:*

Women Seeking Men
40-year-old, pretty, vivacious, classy, fun, DWPF, non-smoker, fit, loves hiking, biking, tennis, travel, Golden Retrievers, nights by the fire. ISO DWPM, N/S, college graduate, successful, sincere, warmhearted, 5'8" plus.
Men Seeking Women
Tall, handsome, complex, successful, 45-year-old. SWM ISO intelligent, tall, attractive, fit, active, romantic 35-ish WPF. Ready to give and receive 100 percent commitment and full partnership with lifelong best friend.

Assuming he can fit Golden Retrievers into a "100 percent commitment" and will budge five years in his search for a younger woman and, assuming she can handle his "complexity," we would hope these two will exchange letters and photos through their anonymous mail boxes at the newspaper and meet. They clearly haven't run into each other by any of the tried-and-true ways: at church, or the office, or in college, or clubs, or through married friends. Those were the old options (before "Personals" and Internet dating services) and they worked.

And they can still work. Even arranged marriages work. Marriages arranged by trusted third parties function much better than the typical union, in which passion is expected to precede and promote commitment. The majority of marriages around the world follow this pattern. Those unions tend to last because couples enter life together with their eyes wide open. Only later do their hearts open as well. So, if you are seriously seeking a relationship that will last (rather than "the One"), consider checking the Yellow Pages and calling a matchmaker.

Men and women who publish personal ads are like fish swimming in the ocean. Unless you swim with your own school of fish, you risk moving alone through the waters and encountering a shark. Matchmakers know that successful marriages rest more on commonalities than on passion. In love, opposites often attract, but couples don't remain attached unless they have a lot in common.

In all likelihood, you don't even know what is uniquely attractive about yourself in the eyes of a potential mate or prospective close friend. So you're likely to concentrate on candidates who promise "evenings by the fire," "long walks on the beach," and "romps with Golden Retrievers" rather than their compatibility with your character, values, and ideals. If so, you are better to rely on matchmakers—not necessarily professionals, but friends who know you well and have a circle of friends and acquaintances with interests in common. Most mature matches begin not with physical attraction, but with mutual interests and beliefs that lead to friendship before love. You can safely leave the passion for later; it will be there waiting for you.

HE LOVES, SHE LOVES

HUGS isn't exactly what it sounds like, but intimacy is its ultimate purpose. HUGS (Helping Undergraduates Socialize) is the brainchild of Brown University student Rajib Chanda: a computerized dating service on the Ivy League campus. The late John F. Kennedy, Jr. was once a Brown undergraduate, and it's difficult to believe that he ever had a problem getting a date. Still, fully one-third of the university's students subscribe to the service. They include athletes and artists, fraternity brothers and rebels, geeks and gays.

Chanda, a fraternity president, sensed that his fellow students yearned for old-fashioned courtship—a way to sample intimacy without plunging into sex. "In a normal Brown relationship," he explains, "you meet, get drunk, hook up, and then either avoid eye contact the next day or find yourself in a relationship."[4] That's neither love nor even passion. HUGS offers the alternative of friendship between like-minded peers that may, or may not, blossom into something more.

Computerized dating services such as HUGS offer better chances of success in romance than running personal ads in newspapers. With a personal ad, you expose yourself to a world of predators at the same time as you take cover behind come-hither copy that could describe countless other men and women looking for love. At any age, a reputable dating service offers a better chance to express who you are, what motivates you, your ideals and ambitions, and what you seek in a partner. Such services match you only with prospects whose profiles complement yours, saving you from some dull (and perhaps a few scary) encounters. Some services offer the opportunity to present yourself on videotape and, in turn, to view the tapes of potential partners. Still, be wary.

It's wise to narrow the field from the outset. African Americans, Latinos, Muslims, and Jews who publish personal ads typically seek others from the same cohort, as do gays and lesbians. But too many seekers specify only height, age range, physical beauty, and nonsmoking as prerequisites. Needless to say, those qualifications hardly speak to friendship, let alone to love and a future together.

If you are seeking a fresh start at finding love, acknowledge from the outset that Mr. or Ms. Right probably also shares your religious beliefs, your cultural interests, and your level of education and intelligence. Your prospective mate will also feel the same way as you do about children and the care of parents. So, before you start advertising your yearning for walks on the beach and evenings in front of the fire, state clearly that you seek someone who affirms who you are and what you stand for.

FRIENDLY STRATEGIES

Success in connecting with friends or lovers requires us to respect differences, accept apologies, let go of the past, tread softly on others' scars, and leave the door open to negotiation and forgiveness after disputes. Intimacy shrivels when we compete with one another, blame each other, and insist on being right.

Outsiders recognize good friends and lovers of both sexes by what they do: They spend time together, preferring each other's company. They share their vulnerable feelings, their hopes, and their dreams. They compliment (as well as complement) each other.

Psychologists warn that anger and anxiety are more intense passions than love and joy. They destroy relationships. So do silence, indifference, and manipulation. Anyone entering a close relationship expecting to change a friend or lover is doomed to disappointment Psychologist Barbara De Angelis laid out *The Real Rules* for women seeking partners, but most of them turn out to be the same ones that bind all close relationships. Here are some of them:

1. Treat others the way you want them to treat you.
2. Remember that the opposite sex needs as much love and reassurance as you do.
3. Choose partners who play by the rules.
4. Don't play games.
5. Be yourself.
6. If you like someone, express your feelings.
7. Ask questions before you get too involved.
8. Don't become involved with partners who aren't completely available.
9. Look for a person with good character.
10. Pay attention to warning signs of possible problems.
11. Judge persons by the size of their hearts, not the size of their wallets.
12. Be fair: don't practice double standards.
13. Don't fall in love with a partner's potential.
14. Be honest about your feelings.
15. Reveal your most attractive feature—your mind.
16. Be emotionally generous, not emotionally stingy.
    The following rules apply to relations between the sexes:
17. Wait until you are emotionally intimate before becoming sexually intimate.
18. Don't lower yourself to behaving like a sex object.
19. Love, honor, and respect—and expect the same in return.
20. Be monogamous, develop a partnership, and spend the rest of your life together.[5]

CONNECTING WITH YOUR CHILDREN

If you are a single mother or father, you need not only to reach out for friendship and love, but to look inward as well to the children in your care. But beware of expecting your child to become your best friend or yourself to be your kids' soul mate. Children choose their own friends. Ideally they will love you, but as a parent, not a pal.

If you are yourself the adult product of a dysfunctional family, you may bear invisible scars. To make a new start toward happiness, you have to find self-esteem apart from your family, stop playing the part of your own parents' child and your own child's best friend.

It is possible to grieve and still forgive those who cause you pain. Tolstoy observed that each unhappy family is unhappy in its own way. If your family situation is dysfunctional, you must acknowledge your complicity in your unhappiness in order to break the spell that was cast when you were a child.

Freed from the spell and the constraints of your family's unrealistic expectations of you, you will not be tempted to heap such expectations on your own children. You can begin to trust yourself, rely on your own resources, and pursue your own values. You will be able to forget about yourself, enjoying others democratically—not simply for the roles that they play in your life. Moreover, you will learn compassion for the less fortunate.

Lamentably, much of modern parenting proceeds from false premises. Alice Miller, in her book *For Your Own Good: Hidden Cruelties in Child Bearing and the Roots of Violence,* suggests some of these heresies that can prevent a single parent from enjoying a healthy relationship with his or her children:

1. Duty produces love.
2. Hatred disappears if we forbid it.
3. Parents deserve respect simply because they are parents.
4. Children do not deserve respect until they are adults.
5. Obedience builds character.
6. Self-esteem is selfish.
7. Tenderness weakens character.
8. Treating children coldly prepares them for real life.
9. The way you behave is more important than the way you are.
10. Parents cannot survive being offended by their children.
11. All strong feelings are harmful.
12. Parents are always right.[6]

Unfortunately, many single parents absorbed these beliefs from their own parents and continue to apply them uncritically on their children. You and your kids deserve better.

CONNECTING WITH AGING PARENTS

For many of us, life has come full circle. Whereas children formerly expected to be solely on the receiving end of care from their parents, today we are often responsible for our aging parents. The lengthening of life expectancy means that many singles find themselves having to care for elderly parents.

What you want to accomplish with an aging parent is to maintain a relationship of love and trust. Most aging parents are fiercely independent in spirit and refuse to be dictated to, especially by their children. As long as both parents are alive, they prize their freedom together, but, when one dies, you may have to step in, not necessarily with solutions, but with suggestions. You and your surviving parent are both singles now.

If you are like most adult children, you haven't a clue about your parents' finances, but it is not intrusive to assure yourself that your surviving parent is protected in your dead parent's will. The survivor may never have balanced the family checkbook, let alone paid a bill in fifty years of marriage, so offer to review finances.

If your parent is hapless about paying bills, you do not have to take over that responsibility. For a small fee, the trust department of your parent's local bank will pay bills, track investments, receive Social Security and pension benefits, and arrange state and federal tax filings. Be sure to make a checklist of your parent's doctor, dentist, banker, lawyer, and investment advisor, as well as the location of any safe-deposit box, insurance policies, credit cards, titles, personal valuables, and checking and savings accounts. Share that list with your parent's lawyer.

Make certain that your surviving parent has a will. You do not have to pry into its details; only reassure yourself that your parent's lawyer has an updated copy on file and that someone has power of attorney to make decisions on your parent's behalf if he or she becomes incompetent. If your parent is reticent to talk about failing health, consider speaking discreetly to his or her doctor to get a prognosis. Don't put yourself in the position of Terry Schiavo's parents and husband, who clashed over whether to keep her alive and whose conflict went all the way to the U.S. Supreme Court.

When my own mother lost consciousness toward the end of a fatal illness, she left no living will to guide her doctor about how much effort to expend in an effort to prolong her hopeless condition. Fortunately, he trusted my word that my mother wanted to be allowed to die naturally, not hooked to machines. It is wiser to ask your parent to give you or a sibling medical power of attorney to make that end-of-life decision.

Because you will always be your parent's child, it will be difficult for Mom or Dad to assume the dependent's role, allowing you to make the decisions. So consider suggesting a third party—someone you mutually trust. It could be a priest or minister, a social worker, nurse, lawyer, or doctor who can better sound out your parent on his or her wishes.

Elderly parents slip easily into denial, hoping for the best even as matters get worse. Unless you live nearby, you will want to know that your parent is covered in an emergency. Buy or rent a medical alert system that immediately contacts the local hospital should your parent fall or become ill. Leave a duplicate of your parent's house key with a trusted neighbor or friend, and keep your telephone answering machine on.

Make sure that your parent is taking advantages of property tax and other tax deductions offered by the county or community. Should your parent run out of financial resources, do not be ashamed to tap Medicaid to cover nursing home and medical bills. Americans agree that we have a right to Social Security and Medicare benefits. Medicaid is no different. Once your parent's savings are gone, there is no need for you to tap yours for his or her final years.

FRIENDSHIP

Even if you aspire to married life, do not neglect your need for friends. Aristotle counted friendship as a virtue and "one of the most indispensable requirements of life." Cicero went even further: "Without friendship," he said, "life is not worth living." Blood may be thicker than water, but friendship is not nearly as burdened by emotion and expectation as family life. Romantic love is, by definition, exclusive and possessive, whereas friendship is open and free. Marriage is bound by contract, whereas friendship is voluntary, beyond legal and formal control. My wife and I each have a best friend. She hasn't seen her friend in years, but they talk to each other on the phone and communicate by e-mail daily, sharing books, gifts, advice, and laughter. Although my friend lives nearer, we too seldom see each other but still keep in touch, bringing humor into each other's life. A friend is a constant gift, and friendship is a sheltering tree.

In 2006, my college class celebrated its fiftieth reunion. Although we lived and studied together for just four years fully half a century earlier, we picked up on our conversations as if graduation had been only yesterday. My wife's grammar and high school classmates gather every year and correspond by e-mail frequently. Surely one of the greatest advantages of the Internet age is that it allows us to rediscover old friends and renew those ties. Don't be shy about reaching out as a voice from the past. Our mere acquaintances abound in our present lives, but old friends count for much more, offering commitment, candor, trust, honesty, and commonality—not to mention nostalgia—free from emotional demands.

In recent years, my wife and I became Friends—the kind with a capital "F"—joining a Quaker Meeting in Virginia. The Religious Society of

Friends includes Christians, Jews, Buddhists, and Moslems, all joined in the belief that there is something of God in every human being. That conviction is a sound basis for friendship.

Church, synagogue, and mosque are traditional sources of friendship, but so too are hobbies and sports. Trekkies, I'm told, make fast friends at Star Trek conventions. But friends don't just happen; they must be cultivated.

BEST FRIENDS

A Gallup poll reveals that four out of five women have a best friend, nearly always another woman. Intimacy within marriage is expected, but it may be overrated, considering that only 13% of married women consider their husband to be their best friend. That is not to say that married couples are unfriendly, but only that marriage seldom completely satisfies the need for friendship that is shared by women and men alike.[7]

When the magazine *New Woman* surveyed 16,000 divorced and ever-single readers, a substantial majority of them acknowledged that, if they never marry, they will devote even more attention to their friends than they already do.[8] Lee Reilly in *Living Single* acknowledges that "friendship is the least defined, the most negotiable, and the most vulnerable relationship in our lives. Without formal sanction, without an established seal of approval or a specific code of behavior, friendship is a delicate thing, often tested and easily overwhelmed."[9]

For all that, making and trusting friends is utterly essential, not optional, for anyone seeking satisfaction in single living. And it demands effort and initiative, but the rewards are incalculable.

At one point in my life, when I lived in Amherst, Massachusetts, I made friends with a scholar who occupied the home where the ever-single poet Emily Dickinson resided all of her life. Tradition portrays Emily as a recluse. However, she enjoyed many friends in childhood and adolescence. But as they married and left Amherst, she complained to one: "I know I can't be with you always . . . some day a 'brave dragoon' will be stealing you away and I will have farther to go to discover you at all."[10] And, in a letter to her future sister-in-law, the poet depicted a dragon who carries women off to a high mountain where they can no longer be reached. Emily sketched herself in mourning dress at the base of the mountain. That was back in the 1850s in small-town New England, when the Belle of Amherst was dismissed as an eccentric spinster. By contrast, single men and women today suffer no such constraints on making and keeping friends, married or unmarried.

Among the great friendships in history is that between lifelong single Susan B. Anthony and the married Elizabeth Cady Stanton—the most prominent figures in America's women's suffrage movement. Stanton, obliged to stay at home to care for her husband and children, complained to Anthony, who was free to travel constantly for the cause. In one letter to Anthony, Stanton complained: "Where are you Susan & what are you doing? Your silence is appalling. Are you dead or married?"[11]

As far back as 1987, a *New Woman* poll revealed that three of four divorced or ever-single women held personal fulfillment to be more important than a good marriage. Fulfillment rests on friendship. Lee Reilly notes, "This focus on friendship may be an edge that ever-single women have over ever-single men":

Women tended to value and seek intimacy and they benefited from . . . a network of people who shared activities and values. [Men's] life satisfaction was much more influenced by self-esteem, by their feelings about themselves . . . Ever-single men seem to suffer much more from the stigma of 'failing' to marry than ever-single women do—even though the stereotypes of ever-single men appear less denigrating than those of ever-single women.[12]

A SCRIPT FOR SINGLE LIVING

Despite the fact that the majority of adult Americans are unmarried, they lack a standard script for single living. Not only do many singles continue to feel their lives to be tentative, but their families and others are often at a loss to know how to assess those men and women who live alone, however successfully.

A woman who is still single in her late twenties to late thirties is assumed by married friends to be unsettled and unhappy, waiting for the phone to ring. Single men of the same age are assumed to be (a) gay, (b) still adolescent, or (c) confirmed bachelors. Either way, it is tempting to dismiss them as incomplete persons.

The high rate of divorce should signal that it is married (not single) life that is unstable and tentative. The married state may still be honored as ideal, but actual marriages fall far short of ideal. Psychologist Erik Erikson postulated that human growth toward full adulthood requires the achievement of a series of tasks, each preceded by a crisis. One of them faced by men and women in their twenties is to make a choice between intimacy and isolation. Erikson assumed that the choice of intimacy would lead to marriage.

But the capacity for intimacy is not at all limited to marriage; it extends to friendship as well. To attract a mate, men and women entering marriage have too often put on a false front and then find themselves perpetuating the lie for a lifetime or until the marriage fails.

SELF-HELP AND SUPPORT SERVICES FOR PARENTS AND CHILDREN

Al-Anon Family Group Headquarters (212) 302-7240. Support for families and friends of alcoholics.

Alcoholics Anonymous World Services (212) 686-1100. Mutual support for alcoholics in your community.

Because I Love You (213) 659-5289. Support group for parents encountering behavioral problems.

Childhelp USA (800) 4-A-CHILD. Offers professional counseling and referrals for parents feeling overwhelmed by responsibilities.

Co-Dependents Anonymous (602) 277-7991. A 12-step program for members of dysfunctional families sixteen years of age and over.

Families Anonymous (800) 736-9805. Self-help organization for families and friends of drug abusers. Local and international chapters.

National Association for Adult Children of Dysfunctional Families (414) 921-6991. A referral agency.

Parents Anonymous (800) 421-0353 (in California: (800) 352-0386). For parents who have abused a child or victims of abuse who need parenting skills. Chapters throughout the United States and Canada.

Parents Involved Network (215) 735-2465. Enables parents to share problems and solutions.

Parents United (408) 280-5055 (Crisis line: (408) 279-8228). Support for families in which incest has occurred.

Secular Organization for Sobriety (818) 980-8851. Similar to AA, but without the spiritual element.

T.A.L.K. for Parents (602) 953-2610. For parents whose children have behavioral problems.

ToughLove (215) 348-7090 or (818) 843-5689. Trains parents to modify their children's problem behavior.

MARRIAGE AND FAMILY COUNSELING

American Association for Marriage and Family Therapy (800) 374-2638. For referrals to local counselors.

American Association of Pastoral Counselors (703) 385-6967.

ASSISTANCE FOR AN AGING PARENT

Eldercare Locator (800) 677-1116). Will connect you with your local agency on aging.

National Association of Professional Geriatric Care Managers (602) 881-8008. Referral to local professionals who can oversee your parents' care when you can't.

Legal Counsel for the Elderly (800) 424-3410. A service of the American Association of Retired Persons.

National Rehabilitation Information Center (800) 346-2742 and naric@capaccess. org. A federally funded referral system.

National Self-Help Clearinghouse (212) 354-8525. A referral agency.

National Alliance for the Mentally Ill (800) 950-6264.

National Foundation for Depressive Illness (800) 248-4381.

Nursing Home Information Service (202) 347-8800 ext. 340/341. A service of the National Council of Senior Citizens.

National Meals on Wheels Foundation (800) 999-6262. Can arrange to bring meals to aging parents or provide group dining.

National Association for Home Care (202) 547-7424.

Visiting Nurse Associations of America (800) 426-2547.

Hospice Hotline (800) 658-8898.

FOR SPECIFIC PROBLEMS AFFECTING RELATIONSHIPS

National Institute on Drug Abuse (800) 662-HELP.

National Cocaine Hotline (800) COCAINE.

Woman to Woman (212) 355-4380. A service of the Junior League.

National Council on Alcoholism and Drug Dependence (212) 206-6770.

Anorexia and Bulimia Resource Center (305) 444-3731.

Society for Sex Therapy and Research (212) 920-4576. For sexual addictions. Your local chapter of Alcoholics Anonymous can also provide referrals.

LIVING WILLS AND HEALTH CARE POWER OF ATTORNEY

National Hospice and Palliative Care Organization. Download your state's advance directive forms at www.caringinfo.org.

5

Cultivate the Right Attitude

"If you aren't fired with enthusiasm, you will be fired with enthusiasm."
Coach Vince Lombardi

Awakening alone to each new day, you can either curse your solitude or savor the fact that the day belongs completely to you. You own it. If you favor the notion that singles are already handicapped as they face the uncertain day, take heart. The mark of a good card player is the ability to win with a bad hand.

When, as a young singer, Tom Jones couldn't find work, he contemplated throwing himself under a train. Fortunately, he reconsidered. Comedian Joan Rivers has made a career of making people laugh at life's (and their own) absurdities. But it wasn't so easy for her to bounce back in middle age from the tragedies in her own life. Over the course of a few months, she lost her television show, her husband committed suicide, her daughter estranged herself, her Broadway play closed, and her jewelry company went belly-up, leaving her liable for $37 million in debts accumulated by its bankrupt parent corporation. Joan's trademark piece of jewelry depicts a bumble bee. Here's why: scientists suspect that nature did not design the clumsy bumble bee to fly, but it surprises everyone. Joan wears her bumble bee pin as a constant reminder that she is not the victim of fate.

Nor are you. There is no such thing as fate. Whatever cards you hold, you can play them. At most, only half of your life's quality is dictated by the facts; the other half is controlled by your attitude. With a positive, realistic approach you can change many of the facts. But first you must face them and see them for what they are. A stiff upper lip in the face of adversity is the way of retreat and denial. Anger and mourning are actually better attitudes. If you don't think so, recall Jesus driving the moneychangers from the temple and weeping at the tomb of his friend Lazarus. If Christ considered strong emotions to be appropriate in adversity, you can too.

FACE THE FACTS

So throw things, kick things. But be certain that your emotion is on target, not aimed at some innocent person who happens to be in the room when you're mad. When you're alone, you'll be inclined to get mad with yourself. Even self-pity is okay, as long as you wallow in your misery sufficiently to get it over with. But don't deny your condition; that's deluding yourself and will only make it worse. Mourners used to signify their grief by wearing black arm bands. Don't wrap a black band around your soul.

Psychotherapist Susan Bodnar acknowledges that denial has the bogus advantage of protecting people from anxiety.[1] But anxiety is provoked by fear of the unknown. You know what bothers you. That knowledge is the key to confronting bad conditions when they occur. Yours may not be the best of all possible worlds (whose world is?), but you can make it better by facing the facts.

The first step is to set forth those facts on paper. Joan Rivers suggests making a list describing your situation. At her nadir, she says she would have written this:

My husband of 22 years killed himself. My career is over. I am a widow, and my daughter, the most important person on earth to me, is now fatherless. Despite the fact that we live in a big house and have nice things, we are, because of bad investments, nearly broke.[2]

(Note Joan's avoidance of euphemisms that might color the facts but only temporarily ease her pain.)

Now write down how the facts have affected you: all of the big and little ways that you are hurting. When Joan's husband killed himself, she lost more than a mate. She lost her best friend, the father of their daughter, her life's partner, business manager, protector, bill payer, driver, and Mister Fixit. By objectifying your pain, as she did, you can learn to deal with it and be prepared to move on and start over.

Pity the mothers of Jewish comedians: they suffer from bad notices. But they are not the only mothers who make their offspring feel guilty. My own mother compensated for the raw deal that she felt she had gotten from life by mistrusting everyone's motives and berating them. Once, in my thirties, when I had just lost my job, my first marriage was turning sour, and my children were all sick, I lashed out at her abuse. It proved to be pointless; her response was to act more persecuted than before. A clergyman suggested that I deal with my frustration by writing letters to my mother, explaining my hurt and exasperation, but never mailing them. The ploy helped, and, after a time, I tore up the letters. When my mother died, as quarrelsome as ever, I was no longer angry at her.

Benjamin Franklin once vented his anger to an antagonist by sending this letter:

You, sir, are my enemy and I am
Yours,
B. Franklin[3]

When Harry Truman drafted letters to critics, his wife Bess read and destroyed them before they were sent. The sole exception was the president's angry protest of critic Paul Hume's devastating review of his daughter's singing. Bess, unfortunately, didn't catch that one, and the president was made to look foolish.

THE WHEEL OF FORTUNE

My mother, who was born to two poor blind parents, never overcame her deprived childhood but kept insisting that life was a cheat, even after she was in comfortable circumstances. Although my father had more to complain about, he never did. His formal education ended with grammar school, and he worked all of his life for the same company, never receiving a promotion. After he was forcibly retired at age sixty-one, he malingered and then spent his last dozen years, increasingly paralyzed, in a nursing home. He often had black moods, but he met adversity positively. He was the kind of man who would stoop to pluck a wildflower from among weeds and wear it all day in his lapel.

Some misfortunes are predictable, and wishful thinking cannot deter them. But they can be anticipated and dealt with philosophically—not stoically, but positively and with a sense of humor. Half of all marriages end in divorce. In any given year, one in five new businesses fails, and one in twenty Americans loses his or her job. Four of every five married women will be widowed in their lifetimes. Of course, everyone gets sick, and we will all die.

But life is something other than the sum of its tragedies. It offers opportunity for growth and enjoyment, fun and laughter. We are all more resilient than we are prone to think. Even after the worst accidents, when people have been injured and their homes destroyed, the survivors typically thank God "because it could have been worse." Armed with a realistic attitude, your disappointments won't translate into discouragement. My wife advises that when life hands you a lemon, make lemonade.

Of course, to be palatable, lemonade needs to be sweetened, so you will have to do something to sweeten life on your own—to become the aggressor rather than the victim. If you find yourself grieving, start thinking of what will make you feel better. Don't be deterred by restrictions that you've imposed on yourself. Over a lifetime, you've created your own character, so it's perfectly permissible to act out-of-character when it's appropriate. Often, that's the key to taking charge of your life: becoming a different sort of person.

My wife's best friend from childhood was served divorce papers by her husband on her birthday; she was set financially adrift in middle age, having never held a paying job. Undeterred, she pounded the pavements in New York, got employment, only to lose it when she was crippled for months by knee surgery. It's her habit at bedtime to write down all of the good things that have happened to her that day and then decide on the good things that she will do for herself tomorrow. She counts her blessings, not her woes. Bad times are the best times to be good to yourself. There are no medals for self-pity—only for courage. Ever since I've known her, it's been my wife's way to greet misfortune with celebration. Instead of settling for heartbreak, break out the champagne and caviar.

GET MAD

Anger is a positive attitude when it is properly directed. If you are angry, it's probably because something or someone hurt you or let you down. That's real. Anger exists for a reason and deserves not only attention but respect. The only bad anger is the kind that we direct at ourselves; that is madness. It's pointless to berate yourself for failure; that only doubles the pain.

We learn from our mistakes, but too often we get angry at ourselves because of an inflated notion of how perfect we ought to be. No one knows what it requires to be a perfect husband, wife, parent, employee, or friend. We muddle through because these are worthy aspirations. When we hurt others by falling short of reasonable expectations, we're obliged to ask their forgiveness. That's only fair. But we must request our own forgiveness first for falling short, and we must give it to ourselves freely.

Understanding your anger will help you improve difficult situations that present themselves to any man or woman living alone. Venting anger is another thing altogether. It seldom helps, especially when it is directed at another person. When anger is used as a weapon of revenge, all that it does is spread your hurt to another person and mark you as "unreasonable" or worse—further isolating you. Nevertheless, if another person is the cause of your distress, he or she has got to be told, and you must do the telling. Swallowing your anger changes nothing and will actually make you even more miserable than you are already.

Thomas Jefferson said, "When angry, count ten before you speak; if very angry, a hundred."[4] The smart rule is not to speak at all when you are angry, but only later. Aristotle was right: "Anyone can become angry, but to be angry with the right person, to the right degree, at the right time, for the right purpose, and in the right way—this is not easy."[5] Anger is not self-righteous; it is a tool for setting things right.

TIPS FOR EFFECTIVE ANGER

Psychotherapist Harriet Lerner suggests these do's and don'ts for dealing with your anger:

1. Speak up when an issue is important to you. Trivial slights aren't worth confronting, but if you feel bitter, resentful, or miserable in a situation, take a stand.

2. Don't strike when the iron is hot. If you start a fight when angry, someone is going to lose it, possibly you. Postpone the confrontation until you've cooled down and have identified the practical solution to the situation.

3. Take time to think over the problem; then clarify your position. Get to the real issue, decide what you want to accomplish, and determine whether the situation can be changed.

4. Don't hit below the belt. Don't demonize the person or situation that caused your anger. You run the risk of winning a battle at the cost of losing the war and never attaining peace.

5. Use the word "I"—not "you." Say how you feel rather than blaming the other person. No one can dispute your feelings, but they will dispute your characterization of them as villains.

6. Don't make vague requests. You can't expect others to anticipate your needs. Tell them specifically what you want.

7. Understand that not everyone is like you. Their values and sensitivities may be different. Things that bother you may not faze them. But people are often willing to be accommodating if you will tell them specifically what it is that bothers you.

8. Don't be righteous. You're not trying to prove the rightness of your position and the wrongness of your antagonist's. Agree to disagree in principle. You just want a solution in practice.

9. Recognize that each person is responsible for his or her own behavior. Don't blame third parties for your unhappiness. Confront the person who is directly responsible.

10. Don't tell another person what he or she thinks or feels or "should" think or feel. The only feelings at issue are yours. You just want the situation to change.

11. Don't pretend to speak through a third party. If you're hurt, say so. Don't allege that your antagonist is hurting someone else by his or her behavior.

12. Don't expect changes from one hit-and-run confrontation. Be patient with yourself and your antagonist, who may test you to see whether you "really mean it." Be firm, but fair. Life is long.[6]

I confess that anger management has been a problem in my own life— so much so that, when it began to threaten my marriage, I finally sought out a counselor, but not until I had turned seventy! You might wish to start earlier. In any case, don't let your anger at others cause you to shrink into your own shell. Remember, living on your own doesn't mean being alone or being lonely.

LAUGH

The best way to dissipate resentment is with laughter. The alternative reaction to any unpleasant situation is simply to laugh at it. Much of life is not nasty; it's just absurd. That's the point of the comic strip "Dilbert." Office politics are nothing like one's personal life. Years ago, when I became president of a foundation and chairman of a seminary, I found myself compelled to compose handbooks for my employees. Of course, without knowing the rules, my colleagues would not have known their rights. But even the best rules, when applied thoughtlessly, can create injustices and absurdities. I much prefer making rules for myself rather than for other people.

Comedian Phyllis Diller had already suffered a broken elbow, facial paralysis, slurred speech, a head-on auto accident, a stroke, and two heart attacks when, at age eighty-seven, she fell and broke her neck in her California home. "I heard the other day that I was dead," she told a reporter. "I played a dying woman onstage recently—I guess I did too good a job," she quipped.[7]

We humans are distinguished from all other creatures by our ability and inclination to laugh. The Vulcan Mr. Spock on *Star Trek* failed to see the humor that is inherent in the human condition, a reaction that was funny in itself. To him, much of human behavior was simply unreasonable. Indeed it is, Mr. Spock, and that's what's funny. Laughing at yourself is one of the healthiest habits that you can acquire, and you can laugh at yourself without benefit of an audience.

Rest assured, you don't have to crack jokes yourself to find humor in your life. By taking yourself less seriously, the burden of being wonderful all of the time will be lifted from your shoulders. Laughter actually releases chemicals that make us feel better. It also contributes to our health. A hundred laughs are equivalent to ten minutes of aerobic exercise.

Laughter will help you to live fully in the present rather than with regret for the past and worry about the future. Consider this free particle of wisdom gleaned from the Internet:

Yesterday is history.
Tomorrow is a mystery.
Today is a gift.
That's why it's called the present.

Theologians tell us that God lives totally in the present tense and that life in eternity is a never-ending now—an inexhaustible permanent moment. If heaven consists of living the present moment to the brim, you can anticipate eternity now! The best way to make the most of the present moment is to be fully occupied. The late comedian George Burns lived nearly to the age of 100 and kept busy to the end. He acknowledged in old age that getting up in the morning was the hardest task that he faced all day, but he relished life because, once on his feet, he was always busy. Boring jobs are the ones that fail to fully occupy us. Choose tasks that demand more of your attention and interest.

When I was promoting my book, *Spiritual Simplicity*, an interviewer on NBC asked me to name a celebrity who lives a simple life. To his astonishment (and my own), my answer was Donald Trump. The mogul with the expressionless face lives simply to work and is always fully employed. I wouldn't want to be so busy, but, ironically, life becomes more complicated the more it lacks focus and initiative.

OPTIMISTS AND PESSIMISTS

Optimism and pessimism are attitudes that get you nowhere, because they fail to reflect reality. It is as foolish to believe that your life will get better without effort as it is to believe that it is bound to get worse despite your effort. Your intelligent investment of yourself makes the difference, and persistence tenders you an endless array of chances to improve your life. When the class of 1953 graduated from Yale University, only 3 percent of its members expressed clear goals for life after college. Twenty years later, those few were earning more money than the other 97 percent of their classmates combined.[8] They were no brighter than the rest, only more focused and persistent. To be sure, money isn't the only measure of success. Vincent Van Gogh sold only one painting in his entire lifetime, but he never abandoned his art. No one dares to call him a failure.

In 1953, at a time when it appeared that the world might suffer a nuclear holocaust, William Faulkner in his Nobel Prize address predicted that, by dint of the resilient human spirit, humankind would not only survive the threat but prevail. With the end of the Cold War, the novelist was proved right. Survival is the best revenge against adversity, and success is even better.

There's just one of you, so beware of investing all of your happiness in just one person or thing. Religious people believe in investing all of themselves for the "pearl of great price." That is the sensible single-mindedness of those who put all of their trust in God. But, in everyday life, even if you're religious, you won't want to place all of your bets on one job or one human being. Loved ones can leave or die, jobs can disappear, leaving you with nothing for all of your efforts. Keep all of your talents fresh and in play, and cultivate a circle of friends beyond your immediate family.

By changing your routines, you will not only emerge from unsatisfying ruts: you will be forced to change your attitude toward other satisfactions. New situations and new goals demand fresh attitudes and approaches. My wife and I have exchanged homes with foreign couples every summer for the past thirty years. It sometimes seems as if we are exchanging our lives for theirs as well, meeting new neighbors, eating different food, sometimes trying out a new language. Each exchange is much more than a vacation. It's a refreshing challenge and an exciting adventure. The very unpredictability of each experience makes us look forward to the next.

SELF-INTEREST AND GENEROSITY

When the United States uses military force or trade sanctions against other nations, it explains that it is protecting its "vital interests." When it offers foreign aid to poor nations, it explains its motivation as "enlightened self-interest," reasoning that Americans will be safer if peoples elsewhere are not so downtrodden that they will riot or resort to terrorism.

In both cases, our nation acts for selfish but sensible reasons. Unfortunately, many people believe that selfishness motivates individuals as well as nations. That suspicion makes us wary of one another. In Washington, disparate interest groups routinely form coalitions to promote legislation that benefits all of their constituencies. It sometimes makes for strange bedfellows, but each organization's explicit motivation is "enlightened self-interest."

In 2007, a Pew Social Trends Survey revealed that fully half of all Americans lack trust in most other people.[9] Married couples tend to be more trusting of others than singles are. That's probably because singles are wary of being dependent on the kindness of strangers. That is all the more reason for you to make friends.

If we believe that individuals are utterly self-centered, we are selling human nature short (including our own). People don't have to be saints to be dependable and to do good. Goodness is not so much a matter of character as it is of initiative and effectiveness. Ordinary people do a world of good.

You will never trust other people if you assume that they are self-serving and secretive at heart. That is what psychopaths and sociopaths think. Doubtless, self-preservation is a basic human instinct, but we are rarely, if ever, so desperate that it becomes our overriding motivation. Most people, including you, are naturally generous. Once you acknowledge that fact, you will become more trusting and more generous and more willing to ask for assistance.

Individual Americans contribute over $130 billion each year to good causes. In addition, 93 million Americans volunteer their time to helping others, working over 20 billion hours a year, worth another $200 billion. Surprisingly, teenagers are even more generous with their time than their parents. Nearly 60 percent of American teens volunteer an average 3.5 hours of their time each week to helping those in need.[10] From the age of ten through her teens, Amber Coffman, a Baltimore girl, distributed more than 36,000 sandwiches a year to the city's destitute. Now a college graduate, she leads Happy Helpers for the Homeless, a voluntary program that has spread to forty-nine states, Guam, and Canada. If you don't already do so, consider volunteering some of your time to a good cause. It's a wonderful opportunity to contribute to the quality of everyone's life, including your own. It will expand your circle of like-minded people, and it won't cost you a penny.

Don't get hung up on deciding whether a beggar is deserving or undeserving of your generosity. Anyone reduced to begging is less fortunate than you. During the Great Depression, the humorist Fred Allen never left home without a pocketful of quarters, and he gave them to anyone who asked. When my wife worked on Capitol Hill, the same homeless man approached her every day for a handout. "Most days none of my coworkers offered me a word of thanks," she recalls, "and none ever said to me, 'God bless you.' But the beggar did." That was motivation enough for her generosity.

ACTING "AS IF"

Attitude changing takes practice. And it amounts to acting, at least initially. Happily, you can write your own script and rehearse until your new role turns into reality. Shyness is an unfortunate attitude. Joan Rivers can command a large audience with her comic routines, but, despite her strident patter, she still admits to being shy with strangers. I handle myself confidently in face-to-face conversations but get tongue-tied speaking on the telephone. Shyness probably can't be completely conquered, but the timid can act "as if" they are confident. In *The King and I,* Anna whistled a happy tune so that no one would know she was afraid. She finally fooled herself as well.

Dr. Joyce Brothers is an exponent of this method. Act as if you are attractive, brave, friendly, and outgoing, and the world will take you at your word. Because of that positive reinforcement, you will begin to be what you intend to be. "But you will still be you," the psychologist acknowledges. "The inner core that makes you special will not change. Nor should it."[11] If you are an introvert, you wouldn't want to become an extrovert, because that would be utterly out of character. All you desire is to become less timid and more sociable.

When assuming new attitudes, you can expect to be clumsy at first, so don't overreach yourself. When I was in my teens, I tried to overcompensate for my shyness by doing stand-up comedy routines during intermissions at our high school dances. My wife readily acknowledges that I possess a substandard sense of humor, so it was no surprise that my life as a comic was foredoomed. If you are shy, don't attempt to tell jokes; instead, start laughing at them. You'll soon find that you have a sense of humor and people will laugh with you instead of at you.

Contestants on *American Idol* require a sense of humor just to survive. They are young amateurs playing at being professional singers before a television audience of millions. Their performances are subject to harsh judgment. All have great ambition and discipline, but they also have the ability to take criticism with good humor.

PRE-VISUALIZATION

Acting "as if" is easier if you use guided imagery. It's a technique that Tiger Woods employs on the golf course. Instead of merely taking a few practice swings before addressing the ball, he mentally visualizes his swing and follow-through and the ball's path down the fairway, onto the green, and into the cup. The famed director Alfred Hitchcock thoroughly visualized every scene in his films before shooting began. When the cameras finally rolled, all he was doing was copying what was already pictured in his mind. The film was in his head long before it was in the can and on the screen.

Surgeons mentally "walk-through" complicated operations before they make the first incision. When my wife, a pianist, was teaching students, she prepared them to perform in public and even in competition. She made all of the students practice, again and again, their entrances and exits, how to stand and bow, how to seat themselves at the piano, and how to hold their hands before they played the first note. Visualizing the entire performance beforehand is a proven confidence booster.

Before I give a speech, I visualize everything that I will do, from getting out of my chair, to placing my hands on the podium, to smiling at the audience. I'm even ready for applause or catcalls before I open my mouth. Anyone accustomed to giving speeches knows that his or her nemesis is the microphone. Mikes are all different, and most are ornery. Not long ago, I gave a sermon in a prominent Washington, D.C. church. Laymen are rarely invited to preach, so I was more than a little nervous even before I encountered the microphone. It was designed to hang around the preacher's neck like a noose. It took me ten minutes of pre-visualization to determine how I would get it on (and off) without choking myself and making a racket.

Your new attitudes have to be tested in public. You wouldn't adopt a new attitude unless you wanted to be more attractive and effective and to make more friends. There's no greater challenge to your "as if" adventure than to enter a large social gathering where you recognize no one. You can't realistically expect strangers to welcome you warmly, because you're also a stranger to them. So you must take the initiative to put others at ease.

Recently, my wife and I were invited to a large formal party in Washington; we swiftly discovered that we knew no one but our host and hostess, who were preoccupied with other guests. It was a party, however, and we were dressed to the nines, so we were determined to have a good time. I grabbed the host, pulled him aside, and explained our predicament. "Introduce us to some people we might like," I insisted. Whereupon he did, and we did indeed like them.

Have you ever seen politicians "work" a crowd, introducing themselves, shaking hands, moving quickly, then slipping out of the room before anyone notices? It may be a slightly insincere variation on the "as-if" strategy, but it works. No one will ever criticize you for acting friendly, and you will make new friends.

OVERCOMING ANXIETY

Shyness and anxiety often coexist. Shy people shrink from the unknown. Anxious people fear the unpredictable. The effectiveness of the "as if" regimen and visualization rests on making the future more predictable. You know how you will act because you have practiced your role.

Still, that knowledge may prove insufficient to calm your nerves. Many of us are nervous most of the time without any special provocation. We're like automobiles with a fast idling speed. Before we can make attitude changes, we need to turn off the ignition. We need to learn to relax.

Learning to relax is not the same as trying to relax. "Trying" is itself hard work, whereas deep physical relaxation is letting-go altogether. When you learn to relax, you will not be anxious. Relaxation and anxiety cannot coexist.

Each Sunday my wife and I worship with Friends at a Quaker meeting house in Virginia. For a full hour, some fifty men and women sit together in complete silence, trusting that the external silence will induce internal stillness and peace. Occasionally, individual Friends break the silence to share an inspiring thought or to read a verse. More often, someone will get up to admit to anxiety about something in his or her life and ask to be "held in the Light" by the others. We are all of us amateurs at contemplative prayer, but everyone achieves some serenity from the silence, because we embrace it in common. People's problems don't disappear, but their anxiety does, and they are able to meet their predicaments more calmly.

You can learn to relax, but you have to devote some time to it—twenty or thirty minutes a day to start. If you exercise regularly and vigorously, your body will be accustomed to the relaxation that comes from healthy exhaustion. Your mind cannot unwind until your body relaxes. Some years ago when I was battling insomnia, I purchased an inexpensive audio tape for that purpose, popped it in my Walkman, and put on the headphones as my head hit the pillow, letting the hypnotherapist's voice lull me to sleep each night. It worked because the voice talked me into being relaxed, asking me to visualize serene situations. After a while, I knew what it meant to be relaxed at bedtime and no longer needed the tape.

A RELAXATION SCRIPT

If you are like most men and women, you don't realize how tense you really are. It's not physically possible to give yourself a full-body massage, so you have to seek inner relaxation instead. Sit in a straight-back chair, close your eyes, and begin making a mental circuit of your body, tightening each muscle group in turn and then relaxing it. First, squint your eyes tightly, count to five slowly, and then relax. Next, grit your teeth and then relax. Then stiffen your neck and let go. Work your way slowly and progressively down your body. You are seeking to sense how it feels to relax so that you can duplicate that feeling the next time you are uptight.

Here's a warning, however: if you are a tense person like me, you may find that muscle groups, once relaxed, actually ache from the constant tension imposed on them. If so, you are so addicted to muscular tension that relaxation can feel worse. The best recourse for tightly strung people is aerobic exercise. You want those muscles to feel like warm jello. Twenty minutes of vigorous exercise three times a week should produce the relaxed feeling that you seek. Once you know how it feels, you will be able to duplicate it simply by willing it.

In her early teens, one of our daughters became anorexic. A psychologist helped her overcome the disorder by putting her on biofeedback—placing sensors on her muscles and then letting her listen to her high-pitched tension through headphones. As she experimented with ways of relaxing, the pitch audibly lowered, so that she knew she was succeeding.

A hypnotherapist once helped me manage my chronic sinus headaches by teaching me this routine: Close your eyes and take a deep breath. Mentally call yourself by name, and tell yourself to relax. Then count down slowly from ten to one, giving a number to each deep breath. After each inhalation, exhale a portion of your tension. Feel your body become warm and heavy. If a count of ten still leaves you tense, repeat the count. Tell yourself that you are relaxed. Imagine yourself to be a leaf falling from a tree, or visualize yourself descending slowly on an escalator. Now picture a massive magnet in front of you and feel it draw the tension from your eyes and neck, from your shoulders, through your arms and out your fingers. It is as if your tension were a thick liquid, slowly draining from your body. Alternately, picture someone else in your own position who is totally relaxed. Then make the circuit of your own body and repeat to yourself two or three times: "My face and jaw feel heavy, warm, and relaxed." Proceed through all of the tense groups in your body. You can't adopt a calm mental attitude until your body cooperates. A relaxed body will.

HAPPINESS

Of course, the permanent change in attitude that you seek when you start over is to become happy. In his Declaration of Independence, Thomas Jefferson inadvertently misled us: happiness is not an objective to be pursued by divine right. Rather, scientists have confirmed that it is but a byproduct of an engaged life. Contented people do not pause to ask themselves, "Am I happy yet?" They are too preoccupied doing whatever it is that commands their attention—whether it be work, family activities, hobbies, or simply doing good for others. Through some still-elusive chemistry, making others happy makes us happy as well.

Francis of Assisi was once challenged by a peasant who had heard of the friar's generosity. "Try to be as good," he urged the saint, "as people think you are."[12] From all reports, Francis succeeded. Despite a life of almost inconceivable self-deprivation and generosity, he became one of the happiest persons who have ever lived.

RESOURCES

Books

Joan Rivers, *Bouncing Back* (HarperCollins, 1997). Highly recommended for wisdom, humor, and sheer practicality. As the author notes in the book's subtitle: "I've survived everything . . . and I mean everything . . . and you can too!"

Dr. Joyce Brothers, *Positive Plus: The Practical Plan for Liking Yourself Better* (Putnam's, 1994).

Christopher J. McCullough and Robert Woods Mann, *Managing Your Anxiety* (Berkeley, 1994).

Harriet Lerner, *The Dance of Anger: A Woman's Guide to Changing the Patterns of Intimate Relationships* (HarperPerennial, 1986).

Stella Resnick, *The Pleasure Zone* (Conari Press, 1997).

Audiotapes

Edmund Jacobson and F. J. McGuigan, *Principles and Practices of Progressive Relaxation*. ISHK Book Service, P.O. Box 176, Los Altos, CA 94022.

Psychology Today Tapes, P.O. Box 770, Pratt Station, Brooklyn, NY 11205.

6

Find and Follow a Faith

Everything is possible to one who believes.

Mark 9:23

To live happily alone requires not only faith in yourself but a willingness to have faith in friends and others on whom you depend for needs both great and small. Faith in oneself begins with self-knowledge. "Explore thyself!" Thoreau urges us all.

You require a further faith—one that provides you with security, even in adversity, and that ensures that you never walk alone. If you were raised in faith as a child, you need to revisit it seriously as an adult. If you are altogether innocent of religious faith, you enjoy the freedom of a seeker. Still, you cannot endlessly flirt with that freedom but must come to some decision.

If you conceive of yourself as a mere accidental speck of life in a vast, impersonal universe, you are not likely to find a faith that holds out much hope for your life's journey alone. Believers and doubters are equally exposed to life's trials, but believers know where they stand in the universe and where they are going.

Rest assured, I am not suggesting that you change your character, becoming "spiritual" or pious if that is not your nature. But you need to believe in someone beyond yourself on whom you can call and depend when all else fails. Adam and Eve learned, to their dismay, that they needed God because they were only human.

THE NECESSITY OF FAITH

Beneath the most fashionable street in Paris, the Rue Faubourg St. Honoré, lie the bodies of 45,000 civilians who died during the Commune, the reign of anarchy that followed French defeat in the Franco-Prussian War of 1870. They perished for their beliefs. Centuries earlier, during the Crusades, Christians died for another idea—wresting the Holy Land from so-called infidels.

In the more than two millennia since the birth of Christ, more than 150 million men, women, and children have died in war—111 million in the twentieth century alone. They were the victims of conflicting ideas, sincerely held. In the American Civil War, according to the *New York Times Almanac* (p. 158), more than 364,511 men perished. Not infrequently, brother fought against brother, but few regretted the beliefs that abbreviated their lives.

Given such a bloody record, it is tempting to regard religious faith as a kind of death wish and to prefer skepticism. But suspending belief is impractical and, ultimately, impossible. We need our faith just as we need food and drink for nourishment and air to breathe—just to get from one day to the next and to make some sense of our lives. Because people's beliefs conflict is no excuse for going through life as a robot, believing nothing. Have you ever met a joyful atheist?

Whatever your age, it's worth scrutinizing whether your habitual ways of thinking and believing correspond with reality. If they don't, they are restricting the hope and enjoyment that you should be getting in your life alone. Beliefs that were adequate in your childhood may not square with adult experience and needs. Faith is important because it is all that we have to act on. No one can live free of faith. If you or I attempted to live confidently on the basis of what we know for an absolute fact, we could never get out of bed in the morning to face the uncertain day. We cannot help but live by faith that falls short of certitude, but we can shed false faiths that are built of little more than habit and sentiment. You can build a faith full of hope—and companionship. With faith, you ensure that you are never alone.

As a child, the great violinist Yehudi Menuhin was such a prodigy that he concertized like an automaton of genius from the age of seven. When Albert Einstein heard Menuhin play in 1929, he exclaimed, "Now I know there is a God."[1] But the boy's genius was also his curse, because he performed utterly without understanding what he was doing. He could play a concerto flawlessly but stumbled when asked to play a simple scale. Accordingly, as an adult soloist, Menuhin was forced to learn, painstakingly and for the first time, everything that had come to him thoughtlessly as a child. It was an agonizing process of starting afresh, believing in himself, but he went on to enjoy the longest recording career of any performer in history.

To lead a confident life alone, you need to scrutinize your biases and unthinking habits of thought and, if need be, exchange them for ones that serve you better. Start with your emotional life. How do you feel about your fellow human beings? Can they be trusted? Should you go out of your way to help others when you're on your own?

Your experience to date has biased you. If you had a comfortable, loving childhood, you are more likely to think philanthropically. If you were raised in mean circumstances, you are more likely to mistrust others. But, whatever your upbringing, if you believe in the Golden Rule, it doesn't matter how people behave toward you, but only how you treat them. That's a powerful belief, even when it is imperfectly followed.

If you have gone through a painful divorce, you may be inclined to believe that no man (or woman) can be trusted in love, and you may act on that faith, despite the fact that it is demonstrably untrue. Weak faith easily leads to disillusion. These days, couples marry warily, and half of all unions fail—many of them because the spouses entered them only tentatively.

CAN FAITH BE PROVED?

Proved? No. Demonstrated? Yes. A realistic faith is one that coincides with experience—not just your limited experience or mine, but the experience of humankind throughout all of history and across all cultures. A valid belief is one that is equally good and holds for you and for everyone else as well.

To illustrate, here is a belief that all Americans presumably share: "We hold these truths to be self-evident . . . That all men are created equal." But hold on! There is nothing self-evident about that statement. To all outward appearances, humans are unequal: some short, others tall; some handsome, others plain; some bright, others dim; some generous, others malevolent. The inequalities are endless. But allow Thomas Jefferson to explain our national faith: "endowed by their creator with certain inalienable rights, among them life, liberty, and the pursuit of happiness."

That's the point. Despite our inequalities in other respects, all of us have rights in common and deserve to be treated with equal respect and to enjoy equal opportunity. Inasmuch as this is a faith, it cannot be proved. But it has been demonstrated that a society such as ours is happier and more civilized if it follows this faith.

Or consider this belief, which is shared by one-third of the world's population: "I believe in God, the Father Almighty, creator of heaven and earth, and in Jesus Christ, his only Son, our Lord." These are the opening lines of the Nicene Creed, composed in 325 A.D., articulating beliefs that are common to all Christians. This belief is neither self-evident nor verifiable by logic—although some argue that it is verified by the Bible, which itself is not self-evident. Christianity is clearly a faith—and a vital one. Demonstrably, it has persisted for 2,000 years and claims more adherents today than ever before. It motivates vast numbers because its tenets afford its believers hope, dignity, reverence, love, and a sense of each man's and woman's unique and honored place in creation. Demonstrably, it is good for its adherents and for everyone with whom Christians come into contact, because they are required by their faith to serve and revere all creation.

A similar validity can be attributed to the other major religious faiths. But to allege that all are basically the same is to diminish their individual genius. Each has been tested by its adherents through the crucible of time and human experience and has demonstrated itself to enrich both believers and the world they inhabit.

The same cannot be said of cults. Some might argue that Christianity was a cult at the outset. In fact, it was only modest in membership. Unlike a cult, it was neither secretive nor exclusive, nor did it deprive members of important freedoms, most notably their freedom of association and conscience.

If you consider yourself a secular humanist, rather than a religious person, you are still operating on faith: namely, that "man is the measure of all things." But if you reflect on people's persistent inhumanity and self-destructiveness, basing faith on human nature alone is difficult to square with reality. Atheism is itself a faith that cannot be proven, but it has serious consequences. If you cannot believe in God, in whom can you believe? Only the demented believe themselves to take the place of God.

ALCHEMY

Some four centuries before Christ, the Greek philosopher Aristotle proposed that one material could be transformed into another by altering the mix of its elements. With that faith, Aristotle became the father of chemistry—and alchemy. The alchemists were fixed on producing a single substance—gold—from materials of lesser value. Many centuries later, as brilliant a scientist as Isaac Newton practiced the alchemist's art. His chronic lack of success did not deter him from his quest or dim his faith.

We now know that the alchemists' quest was foredoomed because gold is an element, a substance composed entirely of one sort of atom and not further divisible by chemical processes into other kinds of atoms. Does that mean that alchemy was a false faith? Not at all. Gold was merely an exception to the general rule. Aristotle's premise was correct, as modern chemistry demonstrates. And we continue to esteem gold.

Newton's faith in alchemy was actually vindicated in the late 1960s, when Judith Temperley, a physicist at the Edgewood Arsenal in Maryland, bombarded mercury with high-energy neutrons, resulting in an atom with only seventy-nine protons, making it an atom of gold! So the faith of the alchemists proved to be correct—only vastly more difficult to bring off than once supposed. According to Barry L. Berman, a physicist at George Washington University, to produce a penny's worth of gold from mercury would take about 1,000,000,000,000,000,000,000,000 years.[2] By contrast, if you choose your faith wisely, it can make you rich every day of your life.

GOLD AND THE GOLDEN RULE

My late mother-in-law, impoverished during the Depression, lost her faith in banks and markets. Ever after, she placed her faith in gold and invested in gold coins rather than in securities and savings accounts. Shortly after I met the woman who would become my wife, I discovered that she had inherited her mother's predilection for gold. When I asked Becky what she might like as a first Christmas gift, she answered: a piece of jewelry. And to be certain I understood her, she added: "real jewelry." So, that year, Santa Claus brought her a small ruby ring set in gold. Even before she knew me, and ever since, Becky has never settled for anything less than the real thing.

It is the same with belief. To be faithful is to be full of faith—true to yourself and true to others. The Golden Rule is a belief in self-worth and mutual respect. If that rule is not yet part of your armor as you face life on your own, perhaps it's because you don't respect yourself enough. The Golden Rule obliges us to love our neighbor as we love ourselves. If we don't love ourselves, we cannot love anyone else. Self-love is not the same as selfishness. There are plenty of people who attempt to compensate for self-loathing by being demanding.

Lamentably, faith takes a back seat to mere sentiment in much of we're inclined to do. Americans are polled to death, asked about how we "feel" or "think" about issues, but seldom about what we truly believe. The reason is that pollsters presume that personal faith is tentative and only a matter of opinion—in short, that we can be persuaded to alter our beliefs.

But in important matters, people resist spin-doctoring, clinging instead to their convictions. For example, a majority of Americans are adamant in their beliefs about abortion, euthanasia, and capital punishment. Strictly speaking, there is no popular consensus on these issues because there is no public opinion. Instead, there is individual conviction about the value of human life.

On your life's adventure, you want your various faiths to mesh. For example, you cannot be at once faithful and misanthropic. You cannot believe in equality and still be racist or antifeminist. You cannot be generous with yourself and stingy with others—or forgiving of self but unforgiving of others. You cannot be at once democratic and elitist. If you are against abortion, to maintain a consistent faith you will reject capital punishment and euthanasia. If, on the other hand, you are pro-choice, then ending the lives of criminals and the terminally ill may be consistent with your beliefs.

Abraham Lincoln noted that, if people don't stand for something, they will fall for anything. For your own satisfaction, you want to be a person of integrity, with a consistent faith that motivates you. Inconstancy is nothing to brag about. Although faith does not automatically translate into virtue, every faithful person confronts his or her shortcomings honestly, as an opportunity for cultivating humility. People of faith neither excuse their shortcomings nor allow their faults to discourage them. We do not demand that our friends be perfect, but only that they be loyal and reliable. Those are the same virtues that they have a right to expect in us.

During my eight years in seminary as a young man, every evening meal was consumed in silence and accompanied by a reading from the *Roman Martyrology*, an ancient book that recounts the sufferings of the early Christians at the hands of the Roman emperors and their agents. The book's gory details would make director Quentin Tarantino sit up and pay attention. But the lesson of each reading was meant not to terrify, but to edify. Here were people of faith who were also faithful, even under torture and faced with brutal death. It is unlikely that you or I will be called upon to sacrifice our lives for our beliefs, but we will live more fulfilling lives for being true to those beliefs and we will prompt people to trust us. Faith is infinitely preferable to fickle fashion or the flavor of the month, and faith begins with belief in yourself, which ultimately rests on a reliance on God.

BELIEVING IN YOURSELF

We humans are the only creatures that possess the ability to override our instincts for self-preservation, laying our lives on the line for our beliefs. Whereas lemmings self-destruct without thought, humans sacrifice themselves with intent. "Greater love than this no man has: that he give his life for his friends."[3] The speaker, Jesus of Nazareth, proved his love by doing just that. All beliefs, of course, are not necessarily motivated by love. But, to be effective, we must love our beliefs. Lamentably, it is often easier to become attached to our faith than to believe in ourselves. Self-centeredness seldom translates into self-respect. Self-loathing is more common than self-respect, and self-pity even more so. Without faith in yourself, you will lack the courage and conviction to start afresh to lead a full life.

Oddly enough, faith in oneself stems not from arrogance, but from humility. Humility consists of being honest with yourself about yourself. Face yourself, acknowledge your flaws as well as your virtues, and believe in your unique worth. Then act from conviction, no matter how often you stumble or how uncertain you are of your rectitude. Over the long haul, it is better to fail for the right reason than to succeed for the wrong reason. Religion, incidentally, is realistic because it both acknowledges our dignity as God's creatures and our need for forgiveness. If you opt instead for a purely secular faith, it must still acknowledge the shortcomings in human nature.

Although people with strong opinions are often annoying, people with strong faith are trustworthy. Because they announce where they stand, we can call them to task when they falter. One reason that politicians are held in low esteem is because many of them do not decide where to stand on an issue until they test the winds of public opinion. Their policies are reeds blowing and bending in the wind. No one can be a faithful spouse, parent, friend, or coworker by playing such a coy, passive, politically correct game. There is little worse than being called a hypocrite.

As a syndicated columnist, I am expected by my readers to be opinionated, but not prejudiced. Faithful people are not shrill, in any case. They wear their beliefs without show or sermons. Self-respecting men and women do not base their lives on mere tolerance, nor do they claim to believe only in reason. Tolerance is, at very best, the thinnest of virtues. In practice, it is often a vice—an excuse for neither believing nor caring. When tied to faith, tolerance can be a practical virtue, but when tolerance substitutes for faith, it is often no more than a wish not to become involved.

Similarly, those who pride themselves on their skeptical outlook, professing to believe only in reason, can be the most unreasonable people in the world. Overwhelmingly, they act from habit, while sitting on life's sidelines professing doubt. They are bereft of inspiration and emotion and resistant to love. In contrast, faithful people take risks, which include being wrong and having to admit as much. St. Paul, so often accused of arrogance, was proud to call himself a fool for Christ. He knew that anyone who follows the example of a leader who was abandoned by his friends and executed on a cross is bound to appear foolish in the eyes of "reasonable" people.

ASSUMPTIONS

We cannot live without faith. Scientists themselves make assumptions that cannot be proved and without which they could not seek further knowledge. Without myths to express our meanings, people could not communicate. The physicist Niels Bohr acknowledged that scientists, like theologians, "are forced to speak in images and parables which do not express precisely what we mean."[4] Albert Einstein concluded from experience that "science without religion is lame, religion without science is blind."[5] With new knowledge, old faiths are revised. But, without faith, there would be no new knowledge.

A vital faith begins with self-knowledge. Shakespeare's Hamlet said of the human animal:

What a piece of work is man! how noble in reason! how infinite in faculty! in form and loving how express and admirable! in action how like an angel! in apprehension how like a god! the beauty of the world! the paragon of animals!

But, in the next breath, the prince's faith faltered: "And yet, to me, what is this quintessence of dust?"[6]

Hamlet's faith in man lacked both hope and love. Although science rests on faith, it can deliver neither hope nor love. Given the opportunity to affirm or revise your beliefs, you want to embrace a faith that has a future and that engages your affections, as well as your mind, now. Each of us possesses an internal universe of thought, sense, intention, and emotion that outshines the most brilliant star. Wish upon a star if you choose, but find a faith that has a place for love, holds out hope, and commands your attention. Thoreau concluded his *Walden* with these lines: "Only that day dawns to which we are awake. There is more day to dawn. The sun is but a morning star."[7]

It is perfectly possible to profess reverence for life, yet still doubt that life has any meaning beyond itself. Such a meager faith seeks no validation beyond itself and aspires to nothing beyond one's personal experience and brief lifespan. Still, there are stoic atheists and agnostics who are willing to settle for a brief place in the sun, who are resigned to ultimate oblivion.

On the other hand, there is a near-universal belief that human fate is not oblivion: that we are creatures of a God who loves us and made us in his image and in whose company we are destined to spend eternity.

However awkwardly and imperfectly expressed, such is the conviction that we exist for a purpose beyond ourselves.

THE FAITH OF SCIENCE

Can such a faith be proved? No. But again, it can be demonstrated that people who hold such beliefs are at once more confident and humble, hopeful and loving, and more inclined to serve their fellow humans, revere the Earth, and contribute to its enrichment long after their earthly sojourn. Believers and doubters are equally exposed to life's trials, but believers, even when they stumble, know where they stand in the universe and where they are going.

Religious faith, of course, does not rest wholly on the near-universal human yearning for meaning and purpose, nor on Hamlet's acknowledgment that mankind, so wondrously fashioned, is not its own creator. All religious faiths take their cue from God, rather than from humans, and are nourished by the creator's self-revelation and his intrusion into human affairs.

These revelations, preserved in scriptures, are remarkably similar across the great religions, although the revelations of each faith remain distinctive. Beware of attempting to become merely "spiritual," instead of embracing a particular faith with its own internal consistencies and disciplines. In matters of faith, you will be assailed from time to time with doubt, but you cannot start afresh without making a conscious decision and then plunging ahead. Against the hopefulness characteristic of religious faith is a hopelessness that pretends to be supported by science. The late philosopher-mathematician Bertrand Russell described "the world which science presents for our belief" in *A Free Man's Worship*:

Amid such a world, if anywhere, our ideals hence forward must find a home. That man is a product of causes which had no provision of the end they were achieving; that his origin, his growth, his hopes and fears, his loves and his beliefs, are but the outcome of accidental collections of atoms; that no fire, no heroism, no intensity of thought and feeling, can preserve an individual life beyond the grave; that all the labor of the ages, all the devotion, all the inspirations, all the noonday brightness of human genius, are destined to extinction in the vast death of the solar system, and the whole temple of Man's achievement must inevitably be buried beneath the debris of a universe in ruins.[8]

Was hopelessness ever painted as poetically as this? To his credit, Russell remained a lifelong stranger to despair. An English aristocrat favored by health, wealth, and a lust for enjoyment, he lived a long, full life, belying his ultimate sense of meaninglessness. Few of us are as well endowed as he was to live happily without hope.

WHAT SCIENCE SAYS

Science paints no such bleak picture of the human condition and our prospects. Scientists avoid making judgments about human values, concentrating instead on how the natural world operates. Even then, science cannot be value-free, because it seeks and values knowledge. Some scientists are more enamored of their quest than is a lover in search of his or her beloved.

Science and religion are alike in this respect: both seek to make sense of human experience. Both rely on a similar faith: the unity, consistency, and predictability of the universe and the capacity of the human mind to grasp reality. Able scientists even share saintly characteristics, being humble before the facts, reporting honestly, submitting their findings to the scrutiny of their peers, and pursuing a quest that is motivated by service to humanity and posterity.

It is often alleged that religious faith is personal and subjective, whereas science is impersonal and objective. But, as the psychologist Erich Fromm countered, objectivity is not achieved through scientific detachment, but instead rests on respect and reverence for the truth—virtues shared by every honest believer, secular or religious. Science and religion alike begin not with isolated facts, but with broad experience, and both seek to make sense of that experience by detecting an order that is underlying the apparent randomness and chaos.

Science would be powerless without the aid of mathematics, which deals with concepts such as infinity and zero, neither of which describe anyone's actual experience. Rather, they are imaginative constructs of the mind. Nothing in the external world, for example, conforms to the square root of -1, which is an abstract concept that is useful in investigating the real universe. The success of modern science rests on our ability to describe the world of sense in terms of deeper and more abstract mathematical concepts. Neither the scientist nor the theologian can understand a fact without a concept, and concepts can only be formed by faith.

Experience is meaningless in the absence of concepts, which alone provide understanding, because they place facts in perspective. To see something is not to understand it. To all appearances, for example, the sun rises and sets daily, rotating around the Earth. It was only through exhaustive and exotic investigation of the movement of the heavens that Galileo was prompted to suspect that our senses deceive us. He began his celestial observations with faith in the regularity of the planets' movement. That regularity could be better explained by assuming that all of the plants, including the Earth, revolve around the sun. No one forced Galileo and his successors to believe in the order of nature, but, without that belief, science would be impossible, because otherwise everything would be random and unpredictable.

THE ELUSIVENESS OF CERTITUDE

Modern belief originated with the early seventeenth-century French philosopher René Descartes, who attempted to describe how people come to a knowledge of anything. In the process, Descartes turned faith inside out. Until his time, it was assumed that human knowledge reflected an objective, tangible world. But Descartes argued that the existence of anything beyond one's senses or outside human consciousness was an unwarranted assumption. He maintained that all that one can be certain of is one's own thinking—or dreaming, for that matter. And neither thoughts nor dreams necessarily reflect reality.

Witnesses in courtrooms often report radically different versions of the same event, substantiating Descartes's subjectivism. I can see only through my eyes and my biases. Looking at the same scene from a different perspective, you may discern something that eludes me, or you may see something else altogether. The various faiths that people maintain reflect the different ways that they view the same reality.

Although you and I are inheritors of Descartes's point of view, we nevertheless insist that reality consists of more than our individual thoughts and dreams. Only a person who is insane is a prisoner of his or her own mind. Sane people believe in the existence of a reality outside of themselves that they can agree on, whatever their prejudices. Science would be impossible without belief in a common underlying reality beyond ourselves. But Descartes and his heirs were correct in this respect: to affirm the existence of anything beyond our own thinking requires faith.

David Hume, an eighteenth-century English philosopher, took Descartes's subjectivism a step further, shaking the foundations of science in the process. Hume noted that it is impossible to prove that anything causes anything else. All we know is that one event typically precedes or follows another. For example, it is my experience that when the temperature drops to 32 degrees Fahrenheit, water freezes. But it is only an assumption that this happens in every instance and that the drop in temperature caused the transformation from water to ice.

Nonsense, you say: it's obvious that there is an objective world out there and that things happen predictably, precisely because one thing causes another. To believe otherwise would be to resign oneself to madness and chaos. I agree. My point is this: these are matters of faith so fundamental that they must be held instinctively by every human being. A proposition cannot be true and false at the same time. You cannot sit on the sidelines of faith and expect to maintain your sanity.

REALITY TESTING

You and I cannot help but live by a faith that is short of certitude, but we may be burdened by false faiths. So it is critical to subject our beliefs to reality tests. At the age of fifty, I experienced what is popularly known as a male midlife crisis—when my beliefs about myself were no longer able to sustain a functional, productive life. The problem was this: my own idealized notion of myself was cracking under a series of reverses. I had failed in my chosen profession and flunked my first marriage. I was caught in a dead-end job, working for venal clients. I was distracted as a parent and inclined to blame my own parents for considering me a loser in life. I was so self-pitying that I lacked generosity and was a burden to my wife. My beliefs no longer supported faith in myself.

In an attempt to regain perspective, I entered sensitivity training, enduring two seemingly endless weekends of extreme physical and mental discomfort, confined in the company of some 200 other dysfunctional strangers. Much of our time together was consumed with people complaining about their lives. It was a nonstop soap opera, with as many plots as people, but what was clear from every sad story was that each of us suffered from faulty faith. Some of us were investing our faith in the wrong persons, wrong careers, or faulty philosophies. Others of us professed faith that someone would rescue us from our own victimhood. Most of us displayed a righteous streak—we were sure of our importance, innocence, and goodness and yet bewildered and resentful that no one else seemed to notice or care. The one thing that we all shared was that we felt sorry for ourselves.

By the second weekend, we got so sick of listening to our own complaints and evasions that we began to confront one another with our lies. In the end, we found it easier to drop our poses than to maintain them. On the plus side, we were forced to accept personal responsibility for all of our beliefs and actions.

I wouldn't wish such an experience on you, but you will profit from some reality testing. On a single sheet of paper, list your beliefs—particularly what you believe about yourself. What kind of person do you think you are? Then ask yourself what you do to justify your faith in yourself. For example, if you think of yourself as a truthful person, what hard truths have you revealed or confronted lately? If you think of yourself as generous, what acts of kindness have you displayed of late? Then summon the courage to submit your findings to a couple of trusted friends. Do they see you the way that you see yourself? If not, do not despair. Your faith may be fine. It may be only your self-image that is faulty. Even saints falter in action, but they maintain their faith despite their personal shortcomings. Your faith ought to be even better than you are—so that you have something worthy to be faithful to.

IDOLATRY AND IDEOLOGY

But beware of becoming the slave of your beliefs. Much of the world's misery comes from people who devote themselves to causes "greater than themselves." Save the whales if you wish, but save your job, your health, your sanity, and your life first, meanwhile keeping faith with people and your creator. The philosopher Eric Hoffer warned that "it is easier to love humanity as a whole than to love one's neighbor."[9]

Be suspicious of idols and ideologies. It is easier to have faith in a crusade than faith in yourself. Devoting yourself to a cause can make you feel good about yourself because it lifts you above your petty concerns. But every crusade has its victims and is fueled by the righteousness of its adherents. Ideologues are notorious for justifying evil means to attain worthy ends. The allure of idolatry is as ancient as humankind. The Israelites found it easier to worship a golden calf than their invisible God. Idolatry is always evasive and therefore a bad investment of faith. Worshipping an image is perverse; you need to revere the real thing.

In the last century, millions died as victims of ideologies that turned their believers into self-righteous killers. Fascism and communism, like all ideologies, advertised themselves as well meaning, but they demanded too much of their believers and ultimately betrayed them. A good faith is not righteous, but honest and humble, generous and true. A good faith claims no victims and takes no prisoners.

A living faith is not just a comfortable perspective on life or a collection of creeds. Rather, it is conversion and life transformation. It will make you a better, more confident, effective, and loving person. As you summon the courage to confront life on your own, start afresh by believing in yourself; then keep faith with God and others.

RESOURCES

No one has the right to force his or her beliefs on you, but it's unlikely that you will come up with a faith that is not shared with many others. Remember that faith is not just intellectual; it is also emotional and personal. It must conform not only with your experience, but with everyone else's. So you have to expand your experience as well as your curiosity. The test of a faith's reliability is the character of its adherents. When you encounter people who are notably better and more admirable for being true to their beliefs, their underlying faith merits your scrutiny.

The actress Gypsy Rose Lee demanded, tongue-in-cheek, "God is love, but get it in writing." Don't expect a signed contract from the Almighty to affirm your faith, but discover more from your reading. If you are a nominal or committed Christian, dip into G. K. Chesterton's classic *Orthodoxy* or C. S. Lewis' *Mere Christianity* (both in many editions), or my own book, *Growing in Faith*. If you are Jewish, you can't do better than consult Herman Wouk's *This is My God* or the many fine books by Rabbi Harold Kushner. If you are intrigued by Buddhism, try Janwillem van de Wetering's *A Glimpse of Nothingness* or *The Empty Mirror*. A popular introduction to the faith of Moslems is *Islam*, edited by John Alden Williams. Among the most articulate exponents of secular humanism are Harold Bloom and the late Bertrand Russell.

When we meet loving couples, my wife and I often ask how they were introduced. Once upon a time, many husbands and wives first encountered each other in church. Their compatibility was both facilitated and buttressed by their common faith. Today, the churches are attempting to adjust to the fact that so many of their members are unmarried, divorced, or single parents—and to provide a ministry that will help them as they navigate life alone at any age.

In general, the larger the church congregation is, the more likely it is that it will offer useful programs for singles. In addition, there are an increasing number of authors who are writing for singles from their own faith tradition. Here are some experts and their titles:

Donna Freitas, *Save the Date: A Spirituality of Dating, Love, Dinner, and the Divine.*

Michael J. Anthony, *Single Adult Passages: Uncharted Territories.*

Christa Ann Banister, *Around the World in 80 Dates: Confessions of a Christian Serial Dater* (fiction).

Anna Broadway, *Sexless in the City: A Memoir of Reluctant Chastity.*

Camerin Courtney, *Table for One: The Savvy Girl's Guide to Singleness.*

Connally Gilliam, *Revelations of a Single Woman: Loving the Life I Didn't Expect.*

Jennifer Marshall, *Now and Not Yet: Making Sense of Single Life in the Twenty-First Century.*

Susan Newman, *Oh God! A Black Woman's Guide to Sex and Spirituality.*

Scott A. Shay, *Getting Our Groove Back: How to Energize American Jewry.*

7

Continue Your Education

Only the educated are free.

Epictetus

When, still in his twenties, Paul Okalik was elected prime minister of Nunavut, a recently independent Eskimo state in Canada, the young statesman wryly remarked, "I'll probably be the first premier anywhere still paying back a student loan."[1]

Many millions of single Americans who have been out of college longer than Okalik carry a similar burden of debt well into their adult lives. Although the United States spends more than half a trillion tax dollars a year to educate its citizens, debt falls heaviest on those Americans who continue in school—after their free education ends with a public high school diploma.

After housing, education is the single largest expense borne by most Americans, single or married, who are covered by health insurance. From our nation's birth, education has been considered the ticket to the American Dream—everyone's chance to get ahead. And this idea came about for good reason: over his or her lifetime, a typical college graduate earns nearly 80 percent more than the average high school graduate. Americans with professional degrees earn, on average, nearly four times as much as those with just a high school diploma.[2] No wonder there are now more Americans enrolled in college courses than in all of the nation's high schools combined.

The bad news is that college has become so expensive that most Moms and Dads can't save enough to see their kids through college, let alone professional school. Single adults burdened by loans don't benefit from these increased earnings until they pay off those debts. The allure of marriage can lose its luster when it means adding a spouse's indebtedness to one's own.

Even singles who are free of college debt face a lifetime of learning. You need to hone your skills and learn new things, not only to remain competitive in your job but to gain the freedom to choose another career more to your liking. Most of all, you need to keep learning in order to increase your capacity to appreciate life. Married couples run the risk of running out of things to talk about. Singles need to learn more so that they maintain interest in life and find new interests.

Adult learners these days are not all residing in ivy-laden college campuses for four consecutive years. More often, they are pursuing new knowledge and skills by alternative means. You, too, can continue your education, whatever your age and financial circumstances are. Unless you have fresh interests, you will not be interesting to others, and you run the risk of becoming bored with yourself.

Despite the nationwide popularity of education, the United Nations reported at the millennium that only one in five Americans possesses more than rudimentary thinking and information-processing skills. Another one in five of us is functionally illiterate, unable even to understand instructions on medical prescriptions. Even many students entering college today are ill-prepared to be successful learners. More than a third of students entering New York State's university system require remedial courses. Students in less-affluent states are in even greater need to catch up with their peers and with the needs of employers.[3]

Learning for advancement and learning for wisdom are not mutually exclusive quests. As a single adult, you want to pursue your opportunities for success without going broke or abandoning your present life's pleasures and responsibilities.

A WEALTH OF OPPORTUNITY

My vote on the two greatest achievements of the last century is for the development of antibiotics and the creation of the public library system. Antibiotics lengthened our healthy lives; free libraries improved the quality of that extra lifespan. Traditionally, libraries have served as the poor person's educator, and the borrowed book as the pauper's classroom. Today, public libraries are not only repositories of printed matter, but network sources of information on every subject imaginable. They are vast, free, democratic schoolhouses that are available everywhere.

Offering free access to the Internet, proprietary data networks, and CD-ROMs, as well as audio and videocassettes, today's public libraries are powerhouses for self-education. If you make a friend of your local research librarian (whose salary you are already helping pay), you may find him or her to be a resource for enriching your life that is greater than any classroom teacher that you ever had. There is practically nothing worth knowing that you cannot learn through your public library.

I'm not denigrating formal schooling. If, for any reason, you failed to complete high school, you owe it to yourself to get that diploma. To do so, you need not return to class but instead to pass the General Education Development (GED) examination—a series of five written tests covering writing skills, social studies, science, literature and the arts, and mathematics. Except for the essay portion of the writing skills test, the examination consists of simple multiple-choice questions.

You can prepare for the examination on your own, using Barron's *How to Prepare for the GED*, which is available from your public library or local bookstore. More than two million Americans have earned high school equivalency with the aid of this book, which includes sample tests. When you consider that male high school graduates earn nearly half a million dollars more than dropouts over their working lives, that should be sufficient motivation to make up for the schooling that you missed in your teens. The GED exam takes a total of 7.5 hours—only a little longer than a single day in school—and makes you eligible for college. See the "Resources" section at the end of this chapter for details.

If you are a college graduate, but you have been out of school for years, you may hesitate to return to formal learning. Granted, you may have to brush up on your study and testing skills, but those are only mechanical habits, not a reflection of your intelligence. Returning to the classroom, you can enjoy the advantage of mature motivation over younger students, who have been in classrooms nonstop since the age of six. Adult learners are serious learners because they choose to learn. Singles have another advantage: they can choose what they want to learn, not just conform to others' expectations.

IS A DEGREE NECESSARY?

If you don't have a college degree but are determined to get one, there are accredited ways to do it that do not even require your presence in a classroom. For example, there is home study and distance learning. Of course, if you are determined to interact face-to-face with a teacher, you can pursue courses at your local community college, leading to an associate's degree or a certification in a professional specialty. Cooperative education enables you to earn while you learn and get a leg up on a specialized career just as soon as you graduate. You can even earn college credit for your life experience, including training in the military and through your place of business. If you have done volunteer work, that too can count toward college credit. The options are many and need not be expensive. You don't have to mortgage your life to earn a degree. All you need is the motivation to make the effort.

Before you decide that you must have a college degree, ask yourself how you will use it. Here's a full, personal disclosure: I have three graduate degrees beyond my bachelor's. Not one of them was a prerequisite for pursuing my careers as a journalist, administrator, fund-raiser, author, and television host. You can enter daily journalism with no more than a high school diploma or its equivalent.

To be sure, I learned a lot from all those years of school, but many of the courses were redundant, poorly taught, and marginally applicable to my work. I've learned much more from life, from reading, from other people, and from on-the-job experience. None of those learning experiences cost me a penny, just some time and attention.

A multitude of admirable men and women have succeeded in their lives without the benefit of a college education: journalist I. F. Stone, inventors Edward Land (the Polaroid camera) and Bill Lear (Lear jet), anthropologist Richard Leakey, longtime *Cosmopolitan* editor Helen Gurley Brown, and philosopher Eric Hoffer, to name a few. One of the most admired men of the last century, Winston Churchill, lacked a gentleman's degree from Oxford or Cambridge. Instead, he entered Sandhurst, a military college, failing the entrance test three times before passing it. In later life, the great British prime minister said of his education that he "just had to pick up a few things as I went along."[4]

The anthropologist Margaret Mead and comedian Groucho Marx shared an aversion to formal education. "My grandmother wanted me to get an education," Ms. Mead explained, "so she kept me out of school."[5] Groucho, a chronic truant, recalled his mother asking him, "Don't you want to get an education?" "Not if I have to go to school to get it," he replied.[6]

TECHNICAL AND VOCATIONAL TRAINING

Not everyone must possess a college degree to pursue satisfying careers that pay a decent wage. Unfortunately, the vocational courses taught in our nation's public high schools largely fail to equip students for real-life careers. The U.S. Department of Education reports that only 38 percent of vocational courses taken by men in high school are of any value in the real world of work.[7] Women fare only slightly better. Part of the problem is that technology advances quickly, whereas technical education lags behind.

Even worse alternatives for equipping yourself to keep up with the changing job market are general-education programs. Close to half of American high school students are enrolled in these nonspecific studies. Almost two-thirds of them leave school before graduating, and more than half of those dropouts are currently unemployed.[8] Those who do find work earn an average of little more than $6,000 a year. Even those general-education students who remain to get a high school diploma are not much better off, because they are ill-prepared to handle any further education, which is bound to be specialized.

Before you jump into a formal course of study leading to a degree, make certain that you need that extra education. A formal curriculum can be stifling when you only need specific skills to qualify for promotion or a new career. I made my way in public relations and fund-raising by learning on the job. I've been an editor off and on since college, but my only course in journalism was a summer workshop in television production (which I've hardly used). When I became president of a national foundation, I had to learn budgeting and financial reporting, so I tapped the knowledge of coworkers. Get the job; then learn on the job.

Take advantage of your employer's or union's offers of training or tuition-paid education. Often, these can be converted to college credit later, if need be. More than 60 percent of all new job opportunities today are the result of on-the-job training. In addition to white-collar opportunities, there are more than 800 types of well-paid apprenticeship programs in vocational fields. Most programs require about 2,000 hours of supervised, on-the-job training plus related instruction either in the classroom, by correspondence, or self-study. Check with the U.S. Department of Labor's Bureau of Apprenticeship and Training in your state to assure yourself that the apprenticeship program that you are considering is accredited.

If you are seeking on-the-job skills rather than a sheepskin, consult Harlow G. Unger's book *But What If I Don't Want to Go to College? A Guide to Success Through Alternative Education* (Checkmark Books, 1998). If you want skills and a degree with on-the-job training, consider cooperative education, in which you shuttle between work and the college classroom (and are practically assured of a good job when you graduate). Write the National Commission for Cooperative Education, 360 Huntington Avenue, Boston, MA 02115, for the name of the college nearest you that offers these earn-while-you-learn opportunities.

LEARNING ON YOUR OWN

The late Malcolm X proved that self-education works. He acquired his education while serving time in the Norfolk Prison Colony. "In every free moment I had," he reported in his *Autobiography*, "if I was not reading in the library, I was reading in my bunk. You couldn't have gotten me out of books with a wedge . . . In fact, up to then I never had been so truly free in my life." Later, when an English journalist asked the African American leader, "What's your alma mater?" Malcolm replied, "Books."[9]

You can be your own teacher, relying on the assistance of libraries, learning exchanges, networks, co-learners, television, churches, art centers, free universities, correspondence study, cassettes, simulation games, and activist groups, not to mention the Internet. Use Google to search for information about for every kind of knowledge; then seek out individuals who have compatible interests and share them. Sharing is the key to a happy single life.

You don't have to pay for education: you can barter for it. Denis Detzel, creator of Chicago's Learning Exchange, started with a telephone, a box of file cards, $25, and the conviction that there were "thousands in my community who wanted to learn something, and also a lot of people with useful or interesting skills or knowledge that they would be willing to teach. Why not match them up?"[10]

Ask yourself what you know that you are willing to share and what you would like to know that a learning partner could teach you. If a learning exchange doesn't exist in your community, you can put a card up in your local supermarket that advertises, for example: "Will teach Spanish in exchange for money management skills." The opportunities for barter are endless.

Speaking of the Internet, you can use "chat rooms" to find learning partners at a distance. People who are interested in the same subject are anxious to share what they know. Speaking of Spanish, Tyler Jones at Willamette University offers free lessons in that language, including sound clips, at www.willamette.edu/-tjones/spanish/lesson2.html. The Resources section at the end of this chapter suggests additional sources for self-education that are available on the World Wide Web.

Other sources of nontraditional education are training programs offered by national associations. Write to the Council of National Organizations for Adult Education, 819 18th Street, N.W., Washington, D.C. 20006, for information. Such organizations include the American Association of Retired Persons (AARP), the Association of Junior Leagues, the League of Women Voters, B'nai Brith, Hadassah, the National Conference of Christians and Jews, the Young Men's and Young Women's Christian and Hebrew Associations, the U.S. Committee for UNICEF, the Red Cross, the AFL-CIO and other labor groups, the Chamber of Commerce, the Foreign Policy Association, and major fraternal and religious organizations. Not all of these programs offer skills directly related to employment, but they enrich you with a breadth of understanding and appreciation that will help you get ahead in the wider world. There are plenty of people out there who are anxious to share what they know with you. As readers of my syndicated column and other books know, I deliver paid lectures to large groups around the country, but nearer home I share my knowledge—gratis—with small adult church groups and via television. If you know what it is that you want to learn, your local newspaper can direct you to lectures and workshops that are either free or that charge only a nominal fee.

INDEPENDENT STUDY

Al Leiter couldn't leave professional baseball long enough to go to college, so he studied for a degree in letters, arts, and sciences at Pennsylvania State University through correspondence courses. Studying on the road didn't prevent him from pitching five innings of the deciding game that won the 1997 World Series for the Florida Marlins. "I'd try to do one assignment per road trip," says the father of two. "Allocating my time has been the hardest part—balancing work and study and fatherly duties—finding time to do it all."[11] But he made it and is equipped to start over in business when he retires from sports.

Consult *The Independent Study Guide* (Peterson's) for the names of more than 100 colleges and universities in the United States and Canada that offer courses that can be credited toward a degree. (Warning: not all of these institutions offer degrees by mail, but the course credits that you earn can be transferred to an institution that does.) Today, more than half a million Americans are taking this path to a degree or certification in a specialty. Educators who once looked askance at correspondence courses are now teaching them!

But be forewarned about any course of study: just because a program is offered that interests you doesn't ensure that it will lead to a career in that field. Higher education is notoriously insensitive to the job market. More Ph.D. degrees are being awarded, even in the liberal arts, despite the shrinking of teaching opportunities. New MBAs are being thrust on the business community when there is already a glut. Although there is a shortage of physicians in small town and rural America, our cities and suburbs are saturated with general practitioners and specialists. Still, more

MDs are being churned out of medical schools every year, all hoping to practice in affluent urban and suburban settings.

The single life offers you a leg up to enter a new livelihood that suits your interests and abilities. But don't mistake supply for demand. Match your learning precisely to a changing job market. Want ads in your local newspaper will give you a rough indication of what is wanted at the moment. For a clearer forecast, consult the latest projections by the U.S. Bureau of Labor Statistics at your public library.

PAYING FOR IT ALL

There are ways to cut the costs of continuing your education or even finding free offerings. However, if you choose to go after a degree or certification, your quest will involve some expense. For varied offerings and convenient scheduling, as well as low cost, you can't beat your local community college. The most advanced degree offered is an associate's degree in either arts or sciences, but you can transfer these credits to a four-year institution offering bachelor's degrees.

But be forewarned: depending on your field of concentration, not all four-year colleges may accept all of your community college credits. My twin daughters each studied full-time for two years to earn their associate's degrees, but each of them needed three more years of full-time study at their four-year colleges to earn bachelor's degrees. The hard lesson is this: if you intend to transfer, predetermine which credits will be accepted.

Correspondence courses range from one to six semester hours of credit and can cost from less than $25 per credit hour to more than $200. The average is less than $100. Shop around for the lowest tuition. In higher education, price does not ensure quality. Remember, few employers are impressed with where you got your degree (or even what grades you received), but only that you have an accredited degree and have the skills to do the job.

Typical correspondence courses consist of five to twenty lessons, each with a test or brief written essay. The final examination must be supervised by someone, usually a teacher at a local high school. Educators John and Mariah Bear like to tell the story of the husband-and-wife missionaries who were the only people on their remote island who could read and write. So their college authorized them to supervise each other while taking exams.

The shortest time that you are allowed to complete a correspondence course is two to three weeks; the longest can be from three months to two years. Most schools do not limit the number of courses you can take at any time.

Incidentally, if you hanker for a law degree at any stage in your life, it is still possible to earn it through private study. Nine states (Alaska, California, Maine, New York, Vermont, Virginia, Washington, West Virginia, and Wyoming) permit it. For details, consult the Bears's book, *College Degrees by Mail and Modem* (Ten Speed Press, 1999) or The Law Apprentice Program (800-529-9383).

MORE TIPS

To keep costs low and to save time, get college credit for what you already know and have achieved in life. Phone the College-Level Examination Program (CLEP) at 609-771-7865 for information. You can prepare for these tests conveniently, using workbooks available at your public library.

You can also apply for advanced standing at many colleges and universities by citing life experience, including work training, military training, and volunteer work. See the Resources section at the end of this chapter. Four out of five campuses nationwide recognize the CLEP examination; three out of four colleges grant credit for courses taken in the armed services. Half of them follow other assessment guidelines. Here's the lesson: don't begin as a college freshman if you can be a sophomore, junior, or senior because of your life experience. Moreover, arrange to keep earning while you're learning.

As any parent knows, finding money for college is not easy, and it is no easier when you seek it for your own education. Check under Resources at the end of this chapter for guides to scholarships, fellowships, and loans. To save time and effort, phone a counselor at your local high school or community college for guidance from an expert who deals with this arcane subject all of the time. If you are a homeowner, you can finance your further education with a home equity loan. Apply at your local bank. Interest is typically low and completely tax-deductible. If you are a young adult and going to college full-time, you might consider joining the Reserve Officers Training Corps (ROTC), which offers scholarships up to $9,000 plus a small monthly income.

In every instance, whether you are flush or just scraping by financially, apply for a federal Pell grant through the college or university in which you are interested. Even if you do not qualify for the Pell because of your assets, your application to this program will be used to determine any other assistance for which you may be eligible. Remember also to consider cooperative education, which allows you to earn while you learn. It will take longer to earn a degree, but you won't go broke, and you will likely be offered a job in your chosen profession when you graduate.

Avoid hiring a commercial service that promises to match you with scholarship money. There is no magic here. Financial aid counselors on campuses do this work for you at no cost and handle all of the paperwork, finally presenting you with what you must pay after any "discounts" to which you may be entitled.

SEE THE WORLD

If you have always been intrigued by another country, you might want to consider studying there. Typically, educational costs are much lower in other countries because of subsidies, and academic standards are often higher. When I studied for a *license* (a post-master's degree) in Paris back in the mid-1960s, my tuition was just $40 for a year's study! The biggest drawback to studying overseas is that you are unlikely to get a permit to work there, so you need to cover your living expenses with savings. Depending on where you choose to study, living expenses can be very modest. Another possibility is to seek work with an American company or international organization in the country of your choice and then take advantage of the local college or university.

Many undergraduates get a taste of the world beyond our borders by taking a semester abroad during their junior year. You, too, can take advantage of these programs, which are sponsored by U.S. colleges and universities but use foreign sites and teachers. Depending on your interests, you could study marine biology in Jamaica, Buddhism in India, women's studies in Poland, rain forest management in Australia, wildlife ecology in Kenya, or Middle Eastern culture in Morocco, Turkey, Israel, or Egypt. You could even spend four months at sea on the S.S. Universe, courtesy of the University of Pittsburgh, studying foreign cultures as you circle the globe.

Be forewarned that programs sponsored by American colleges and universities in foreign countries charge U.S. tuition rates—not the lower tariff that you would enjoy if you lived on the foreign economy.

Before leaving the subject, I must mention the extraordinary study programs sponsored by Elderhostel for older Americans all around the world. For example, through Elderhostel, you can study Shakespeare in Stratford-on-Avon with Oxford and Cambridge professors or tour Roman antiquities in Turkey. Each tour is prepackaged at lowest cost, including inexpensive housing, often in university dormitories. There are literally hundreds of offerings in the United States and around the world for men and women aged fifty-five or more who crave education and adventure at low cost. Contact Elderhostel at 75 Federal St., Boston, MA 02110

(617-426-7788) and request a current catalog. International travel can be daunting for singles at any age. The Elderhostel experience offers security and sociability that are superior to what you could experience when traveling alone.

RESOURCES

As you enhance your skills and appreciation through study, the best friend you can make is the research librarian at your local public library. Don't try to stay afloat in a sea of information when a free specialist can steer you to precisely what you need. Having said that, here are some vital resources.

FINANCIAL AID

U.S. Department of Education: http://easi.ed.gov. A collaborative site joining government, business, and education leaders to assist your search.

Federal Student Aid Information Center: 800-333-INFO.

National Association of Student Financial Aid Administrators: www.finaid.org/. Includes sources for 200,000 scholarships, fellowships, grants, and loans.

CORRESPONDENCE COURSES AND DISTANCE LEARNING

Council of National Organizations for Adult Education: 819 18th St., N.W., Washington, D.C. 20006. Connects you with thousands of training programs offered by national associations of all kinds.

National Home Study Council: 1601 18th St., N.W., Washington, D.C. 20009. Ask for a free directory of accredited home study schools.

National University Extension Association: 1 Dupont Circle, N.W., Washington, D.C. 20036. Write for a catalog of college and university correspondence courses and a booklet on home study.

Council of Better Business Bureaus: 1150 17th St., N.W., Washington, D.C. 20036. Ask for the booklet *Tips on Home Study Schools*.

John and Mariah Bear, *College Degrees by Mail and Modem* (Ten Speed Press, 1999).

The Independent Study Catalog (Peterson's Guides, latest edition).

Alternative/Distance Learning: www.yahoo.com/Education/Alternative/Distance Learning.

For law degrees: The Law Apprentice Program (800-529-9383).

The National Distance Learning Center: 502-686-4556.

United States Distance Learning Association: 510-820-5562.

Educational Resources Information Center (ERIC), ericicr.syr.edu, contains practically everything you want to know about anything.

COOPERATIVE EDUCATION (EARN WHILE YOU LEARN)

National Commission for Cooperative Education, 360 Huntington Ave., Boston, MA 02115. Represents more than 300 outstanding two- and four-year colleges that combine classroom study with on-the-job training and experience.

CHOOSING A COLLEGE

The College Guide: www.jayi.com/jayi/ACG. Everything that you want to know, plus the assistance of an admissions "guru."

College and University Home Pages: www.mit.edu/people/cdemello/univ.html. Will take you to the Web sites of all campuses that maintain homepages on the Internet.

CREDIT FOR WHAT YOU ALREADY KNOW

College-Level Examination Program (CLEP): 609-771-7865. More than nine of every ten colleges and universities offer advanced placement based on your performance on these tests.

Council for Adult and Experiential Learning: 243 S. Wabash Ave., Suite 800, Chicago, IL 60604. Evaluates your work and accomplishments for advanced placement.

Non-Collegiate Sponsored Instruction: American Council on Education, 1 Dupont Circle, N.W., Washington, D.C. 20036. 202-939-9433. Ask for information about the PONSI process for acceptance of college credit.

Credit for Military Training and Volunteer Work: Write to 1 Dupont Circle, N.W., Suite 680, Washington, D.C. 20036 and ask for *College Degrees Without Classrooms #2122.*

TRADE SCHOOLS AND APPRENTICESHIPS

Accrediting Commission of Career Schools and Colleges of Technology: 2101 Wilson Blvd., Arlington, VA 22201. Check to be sure that the trade school of your choice is accredited. Also call the local Better Business Bureau.

The National Apprenticeship Program, a booklet available from the Bureau of Apprenticeship and Training, Manpower Administration, U.S. Department of Labor, Washington, DC 20212.

STUDY ABROAD

American Institute for Foreign Study: 800-727-AIFS.

Gail Ann Schlachter and R. David Weber, *Financial Aid for Training and Study Abroad* (Reference Service Press, latest edition).

Gregg Tannen and Charley Winkler, *The Student's Guide to the Best Study Abroad Programs* (Pocket Books, latest edition).

GETTING YOUR HIGH SCHOOL DIPLOMA

Phone your local high school and ask where and when the General Education Development (GED) Examination is given near you. After passing five tests, you will be awarded a High School Equivalency Certificate that qualifies you for college. To prepare for these tests, consult *Barron's Introduction to the GED Examination* in most public libraries.

8

Look Good and Feel Good

God has given you one face, and you make yourselves another.

Shakespeare, Hamlet

Living on your own, you may be keeping your mind alert, but you will be tempted to let your looks slide. After all, you may rationalize, why take the time and effort to appear attractive when there is no one in particular that you are trying to attract?

For an answer, pick up any supermarket tabloid, which specializes in revealing how celebrities look when they think nobody is looking. The candid camera is not kind when its subject has let himself or herself go, even briefly. Take a long look at the photo on your driver's license or passport. Is that the person you want others to see when they meet you for the first time?

For some reason, smiles have gone out of style. To judge by the photos of authors on the dust covers of the books that I read nowadays, most look like a truck just ran over their cats. Fashion models cultivate poker faces. Except for the rare tight grin at sign-off, television network news anchors keep straight faces as well. It is as if a smile would threaten the essential seriousness of life.

"There's daggers in men's smiles," Shakespeare's Macbeth warns us, and his Hamlet cautions that "One may smile, and smile, and be a villain." Nevertheless, a smile is the simplest and most effective way to make yourself more attractive. It is the first step in ensuring that your appearance will be pleasing to others—and to yourself as well. It's all about attitude.

Oscar Wilde wryly noted that "It is only shallow people who do not judge by appearances."[1] We can't honestly blame our creator or our parents for our appearance, because we are largely in charge of the way we look, sound, smell, and carry ourselves. Attractive people make themselves so. In the process, they gain self-respect and confidence, and they attract other attractive people to them. All successful people define themselves, beginning with appearance. Even plain monarchs manage to look regal. Beauty and handsomeness are not just skin deep but a reflection of the way we feel about ourselves. So feel good and look good.

LOOK IN A MIRROR

What do you see? Psychologists have long known that forcing a person to look at himself or herself can be the first step toward rehabilitation. Drug abusers and alcoholics who look like the wrath of God after their benders are sometimes placed in cells with mirrored walls where their degradation is inescapably apparent to them. Instead of retreating into their shells and wallowing in self-pity, they are forced to see how they look to others. The effect is often therapeutic. They are shocked into improving their appearance and their habits. Want to lose weight? Instead of purchasing exercise equipment, Iowa State University psychologists advise you to hang a mirror on your refrigerator.

How good do you have to look? In the classic film *Dark Passage*, Humphrey Bogart hid out in Lauren Bacall's apartment until he could remove the bandages that a plastic surgeon had wrapped around his head following an operation to alter his appearance. We have no notion of what the film's hero looked like before going under the knife, but, when the bandages came off, *voilà*: he looked just like Humphrey Bogart—clearly not one of the world's most beautiful people. Even as a child, I wondered why anyone would submit to a painful and expensive operation only to emerge with Bogie's face. Of course, that fine actor's face was not his fortune. Then again, my face is not my fortune either, and you may feel the same about yourself. But good appearance consists not merely of possessing a pretty face. Bogie made himself attractive in other ways, and we can emulate his example.

Animals do not need clothing, accessories, or cosmetics to enhance their physical attractiveness. If you ever saw photos of nudists as an adolescent, you may have felt a brief sexual rush, but, as soon as your brain took over, it affirmed what we all know—that the human animal looks lots more attractive with clothes on. If you can't choose your body, you can choose its wrappings.

CONTRIVANCES

What this confirms is the good news that human beauty is, to a large extent, contrived. Which means that anyone willing to exert a little effort can be more attractive. There are opportunities galore, limited only by your own estimation of how you could look better. Aye, there's the rub: although many men and women aren't particularly happy with what they see in the mirror, they don't quite know what changes would really be enhancements.

A woman's hairstyle, for example, is the easiest of her features to alter, which explains why hair salons used to be called "beauty parlors." But whom can you trust to tell you which hair style will enhance rather than simply alter your appearance? Professional stylists complain that their customers insist on a cut or hair color worn by some television or movie star that they admire, whether or not it suits their facial shape or coloring.

"Are you sick of looking in the mirror—and seeing the same old you?" the *National Enquirer* asks its readers. That question is the supermarket tabloid's come-on to enter a contest, whose winners receive complete makeovers. The *Enquirer's* annual "New Me" contest for women offers head-to-toe transformations that can be maintained by the winners' own efforts. I'm looking right now at the "before" and "after" photos of recent winners. They do look better "after," but the most obvious improvement is that they are now smiling.

BAD HABITS

I can't recall ever seeing a photo of the late Princess Diana chewing her fingernails, but it was her habit to chew them to the bloody quick, an expression of her insecurity during her royal marriage. It was only after beginning divorce proceedings that she gained the self-confidence to conquer the habit. Researchers at the University of North Dakota have failed to identify a single man or woman who is entirely free of bad habits. They confirm that the typical American is burdened by seven unattractive habits.[2]

Nervous habits are physical: nail biting, teeth grinding, hair twisting and pulling, and throat clearing. "People tend to develop nervous habits when they want to escape from a stressful situation," explains psychiatrist Raj Persaud of London's Maudsley Hospital.

Psychiatrists favor "aversion therapy" to cure bad habits, placing sufferers in front of mirrors so that they are forced to confront the ugliness of what they do thoughtlessly. Relaxation techniques, including self-hypnotism, can relieve both boredom and anxiety. If you are a nail biter, sit on your hands or keep them busy somewhere away from your mouth. At least half of the effort to become more attractive consists of eliminating unattractive behavior.

BEAUTY AND THE BEAST

In his book about the wisdom conveyed to children by fairy tales, *The Uses of Enchantment*, the psychiatrist Bruno Bettelheim affirmed that "It is, in the final analysis, love which transforms even ugly things into something beautiful."[3] It was love, after all, that transformed both beast and frog into handsome princes. Just as we imagine a thin person struggling to emerge from every overweight man or woman, there is an attractive person seeking to escape from every facade of plainness and even ugliness. The French have an expression—*joli laid*—to describe someone very plain who manages at the same time to impress us as attractive. Think of Audrey Tatou or Gerard Depardieu.

Many philosophers suspect that beauty is an altogether human invention and apparent only to us among God's creatures. A peacock preens, a bird calls sweetly, and a buck competes—all to attract mates, but there is little evidence that they are motivated by beauty. Honey is sweet to the bear, and nectar to the bee, but the lilies of the field appear sublime only to humans.

DIETING

The National Institutes of Health affirm what many of us realize already: most Americans are overweight. Government scientists are interested only in the effect that the extra pounds have on our health, but the rest of us are more concerned about the effect of weight on our appearance. Accordingly, Americans spend more than $80 billion each year on diets—nearly the entire gross national product of Belgium. Yet experts agree that the failure rate of diets is 95 percent. Crash diets work temporarily, but the weight goes back on with a vengeance after six months.

Here's a reality check: weight loss, even when successful, leaves men and women with the basic body shape that they have always had. The human skeleton remains the same no matter how much flesh it carries. A long-waisted, big-hipped, wide-shouldered, and short-necked woman will not look like a runway model even if she loses enough weight to fit into a size 4 dress. But take heart: as we reach middle age, most of us actually look better carrying a few extra pounds.

Human beings are the only animals that deny themselves food when hungry. A film star can lose weight temporarily by means of a crash diet—just long enough to shoot the next picture, which is all that matters. That's the slim person we see on the screen. But the body learns to compensate for its denial. That is not to say that you cannot become trimmer, but it will not be accomplished over the long run by starving yourself, taking drugs, eating boring foods, or denying yourself the occasional "fattening" treat. The only regimen that works is to consume fewer calories consistently. That means continuing to enjoy your food, only less of it.

Oscar Wilde sagely warned that "The only way to get rid of temptation is to yield to it. Resist it and your soul grows sick with longing for the things it has forbidden itself."[4] It is natural to get hungry and equally natural to satisfy your hunger in the most satisfying ways.

THINKING SENSIBLY ABOUT EATING

The only effective diet is in your head, not in your stomach. It requires changing the way you think about food. Rather than follow fashions in weight loss, here are some fundamentals:

1. Eat only when you are physically hungry. Hunger is natural. Your body tells you that your stomach is empty, just as the fuel gauge on your car tells you when it needs gas to keep going. Drivers typically fill up at the gas pump when the tank is nearly empty, whereas overweight people keep "topping off" stomachs that are already full. If you have a weight problem, wait until you feel hungry before you eat again, and then think of something that would really satisfy you, not just fill an empty space. Often you are not really hungry, but just thirsty. On those occasions, drink something or chew gum; don't eat. Water contains zero calories and is healthy for you.

2. Stop eating as soon as you are no longer hungry. It's the extra fuel that we don't need that the body stores as fat. Eat a variety of healthy foods, but pleasing ones. Don't eat a carrot when you really want ice cream. But don't eat anything after satisfying your hunger. The human stomach is only as large as a clenched fist. Look at your plate. Is there more on it than a fistful? Take your time eating. You're not taking on cargo or on deadline. You're enjoying yourself. You're not "on a diet."

3. Think thin. Our minds can play tricks on us. Anorexics look in the mirror and see fat even when they are skeletal. But our bodies can play tricks on us as well. If we think of ourselves as fat, that thought is stressful, and stress releases insulin, which turns nutrients into fat. By simply worrying about weight, we think ourselves fat. Stop weighing yourself. Think of food as health-giving—something you enjoy that is also good for you. Skipping meals is a bad idea. It actually lowers your metabolic rate so that more of what you consume in the course of other meals will produce fat. Breakfast is important to kick-start your metabolism for the rest of the day. If hunger gnaws at you before normal

mealtimes, do as slim athletes do—skip full meals altogether in favor of several nutritious (but delicious) mini-meals throughout the day. That way, you will seldom be hungry and your metabolism will be consistently high.

LOOKING GOOD

Physical attractiveness does not conform to rigid standards but is composed of many facets. Each of us can look good in our own unique way. The actress Kate Winslet provides an example. A woman who likes her body and moves with self-assurance and grace is attractive. But before starting to change her body, she needs to establish a body image. More than 80 percent of traditional societies in the world consider prominent hips and legs to be more attractive in women than model thinness. Winslet is happy with her body, and audiences respond to her self-image.

As for men, I like the late Cary Grant's admission that, in real life, he always aspired to be like the Cary Grant of the movies but couldn't manage it. But by his charm, his voice, his sense of humor, and the way he carried himself, he managed to be attractive until his dying day.

YOUR VOICE

If you are an American male over the age of thirty, I bet you can manage a pretty fair imitation of Cary Grant—not the late actor's looks, but his voice. It was a voice entirely contrived by Archie Leach (Cary's real name), who came to the States with a lower-class English accent. Archie learned to speak like Cary Grant, acquiring a rich, distinctive, deep, and attractive voice and manner. An attractive voice is fairly easy to acquire and will last long past your youthful good looks. A confident, resonant voice commands attention and respect. People will listen to you.

ABC's Sam Donaldson once entertained my wife over dinner with tales of his childhood in Texas and New Mexico. When Sam, in his teens, expressed his ambition to be a radio disc jockey in El Paso, his widowed mother insisted that he learn to speak correctly. So she sent him to learn elocution from an actress who had retired from the Broadway stage, with the result that today you'd be hard-pressed to detect Sam's roots in his speech.

Retired NBC anchor Tom Brokaw broke into radio in his native South Dakota, developing a commanding voice despite a lisp. A lisp is also part of Barbara Walters's charm, and it makes her voice distinctive. Dan Rather, the retired CBS anchor, is another rural Texan who learned to speak the universal language of radio and television. Peter Jennings betrayed his north-of-the-border upbringing with a few stray Canadian pronunciations, but his was a voice that demanded that whatever he said be taken seriously.

Actors and actresses not only look good—they sound good. One of the most positive things that you can do is to go to your local public library and check out an audiocassette course in voice training. A deeper, more animated voice will get you taken more seriously and will make you more attractive.

POTBELLIES AND PROSTATES

Let's face it: men have it easier than women. We're not really expected to be physically attractive—only clean and well-groomed. But we have our own problems. Baldness is one of them. The fact is that 85 percent of baldness is genetic, and it can be inherited through both parents. In his twenties, Britain's handsome Prince William already appears to have inherited his father's male pattern baldness. Most men my age just live with it, but younger men may want a second chance at being hirsute. Minoxidil, the active ingredient in Rogaine, works best for men in their twenties whose hair loss has a history of fewer than five years. Unfortunately, the drug requires daily applications for a lifetime. It does not restore a receding hairline, and, at best, only one in three users enjoys a doubling of hair density.

There are alternatives. A complete scalp transplant can cost up to $15,000. It looks natural and can be permanent. If only a bald spot bothers you, a hair-lift is all that is needed, at a cost of up to $5,000. The bald spot is surgically removed and a part of your scalp with hair is stretched over the area. A hair weave is just what it sounds like: someone else's hair is woven into yours to make it look thicker. It is the least expensive option (several hundred dollars), but it requires frequent adjustment. Toupees or hairpieces, long the subject of ridicule, are now much improved. They do not blow off in a breeze, and the hairline looks more natural. They cost $1,000 and up.

Before a single man at any age reverts to such measures, he should ask himself whether he needs a full head of hair. Actor Bruce Willis, realizing that he was progressively balding, decided to shave his head, and his career has not suffered.

The average American man in his baby boomer years is five-foot-ten inches tall, but feels even shorter. The reason is that Hollywood and television now project a much taller man as "average." The typical department store male dummy is no longer a 38 regular (my size at five-foot-nine) but stands six-foot-two with a 42-inch chest and sports a size 42 suit. Don't be depressed: you're being compared to a fantasy. The same is true of women. Size 10 is where real women's bodies start, not down there in the single digits. It's all a vicious fashion plot to make the rest of us feel inadequate.

Psychologist Mark Leary of Wake Forest University advises men to look their chronological age. If you are uncertain about your appearance, ask a woman friend what she thinks. "If she is honest and says no, she doesn't have a problem with it, then you have to ask yourself why you are creating a problem in your mind."[5]

FROM HEAD TO TOE

Your appearance starts with your attitude. Some people in your life will never take you as seriously as you deserve to be taken, but no one will take you more seriously than you take yourself. Designer Karl Lagerfeld chooses his models on attitude, not on looks. Interviewing a prospective runway model, he asked, "Can you walk?" "Well I got here, didn't I?" she snapped. She was hired.

Joan Collins laments that she moped around with a bad attitude throughout her teens, chronically complaining that she had nothing interesting to do. Her exasperated mother gave her this lesson in life: "People who are bored are boring." The actress now admits that "with so many things to see and do, it is a sin to be bored."[6] Interested men and women are interesting and therefore attractive to others.

An aging Tallulah Bankhead used to complain, "They're not making mirrors the way they used to."[7] But you may not be the best judge of what you see in your own mirror. Jean de la Bruyère insisted that "there are no ugly women; there are only women who do not know how to look pretty."[8]

So get help. A complete makeover is unnecessary, but, if you choose to get one, you will be able to incorporate the lessons that you've been taught from then on without buying expensive cosmetics. It's the final composite picture that matters, not the paints that you use. For starters, get a free consultation at the cosmetics counter of a large department store. You'll be pressured to buy a few of the items that have been used on your face. But, if you like the look, you can switch to inexpensive brands.

When I was a boy (and still had hair), I was struck by how many of the barbers that I visited were bald. It seemed to be bad advertising for the profession. A good rule of thumb for women is to choose a cosmetologist who has an attractive sense of herself. If she can make herself look good without looking contrived, chances are that she can help you too.

CLOTHING

Observe shoppers at the mall. Why is it that the clothes that look so attractive on manikins in store windows often look awful on real people? The reason appears to be that we don't know what looks good on us. Ironically, people (the live ones, I mean) dress attractively at funerals and memorial services, because those are occasions when they wear basic apparel. But even the basics must fit well to enhance your appearance. You need a few classic clothes that fit perfectly. It's more economical than buying a bunch of trendy clothes off the rack that you seldom wear. The classics will last you a lifetime.

Dress for your body as it is, not as you would like it to be. Keep it simple. Choose standards in the same color so that you can mix and match. Combine quality basics with inexpensive accessories. Fashion consultant Linda Dano believes a basic wardrobe doesn't have to be much larger than what you would pack in one or two bags to go on vacation.

CLEOPATRA'S NOSE

"If Cleopatra's nose had been a little shorter," the philosopher Pascal suggested, "the whole face of the world would have been changed."[9] Pascal argued that a plain Cleopatra wouldn't have caused nearly as much mischief as the comely queen of the Nile.

You probably don't want to change the face of the world, but perhaps you've considered changing your own face through cosmetic surgery. Surgery is an expensive option, but cost doesn't appear to deter people of even modest means. One-third of Americans who go under the knife have family incomes of less than $30,000 a year.

Before you consent to the knife, however, reflect that even Cleopatra was not a natural beauty. Coins of the time show her to have had a large mouth and a hooked nose. Yet she captivated Caesar and Antony. Plutarch said that the charm of her presence was irresistible and laid all who associated with her under its spell. It was her mind and intellect, not her face, that captivated her lovers. The highly educated and competent queen was a delightful conversationalist and companion.

If you are attractive in other respects, people will actually come to think of you as physically attractive as well. In a recent experiment, researchers brought a group of strangers together for an hour a day, over four days. After each session, the subjects were asked to rate each other's appearance. By the fourth day, they all rated each other more highly. Simple familiarity and likability translated into beauty.

Experts agree that plastic surgery, however successful, will not necessarily change others' opinion of you. Surgery cannot make up for inadequate education or skills. Most goals in life require behavioral rather than cosmetic changes. A new face will not make you more assertive or less shy.

Improving your appearance need not cost a bundle. A smile costs nothing more than a little muscle strain. If you have a problem with posture, consider visiting a chiropractor for analysis. It's awkward to be a two-legged animal, standing and moving upright for a lifetime. Misalignments can be corrected and chronic discomfort can be eased without surgery. You will be more prone to smile once you are feeling better. With attention, you will look and feel more attractive, making it a delight to know you and to be you. But you will also have to look after your underlying health.

LIVE LONG AND PROSPER

Living on your own, you are totally responsible for ensuring the quality of your life. There's no mother or spouse to nag and nurse you.

Modern medicine has provided the means to live long and to prosper—but only if you take advantage of the advances and develop good health habits. Life expectancy has risen by more than 50 percent since 1920.[10] Infectious diseases have been largely controlled by a combination of public sanitation, antibiotics, and inoculations. Heart surgery and organ transplants have literally given millions of our fellow citizens a new lease on life.

You have an array of opportunities for enjoying a long, vigorous, and relatively pain-free life. It all starts with your determination to look after your health and continues with finding a dependable doctor who is interested in your total well-being, not just the symptoms that you complained about on your last visit. Finally, it's a matter of nutrition, exercise, sufficient rest, and a positive attitude—all of those things that your mother nagged you about when you were a child. Now that you're on your own, you must nag yourself.

TAKING CHARGE OF YOUR LIFE

Happy people live longer, and you alone are in charge of your happiness. But when you are ill, you need your doctor's counsel and care. Demand it.

Still, to stay well you must also be your own physician, dispensing prescriptions that include sleep, diet, and exercise, along with positive thinking, steady breathing, proper posture, a calm mind, and frequent laughter. Contentment is good medicine. Joy is even better. Love is the very best prescription. If you have your health, you may not have absolutely everything, but you have a foundation on which to build a satisfying life from there on out. Lesser alternatives aren't worth contemplating.

You must take charge of your health so that you can be in control of every other aspect of your life. Let's admit it: being healthy feels good! It's a gift that we deserve from ourselves. "Wellness" is not just the absence of illness, but the positive pursuit of contentment.

PAIN, PAIN, GO AWAY

Biotechnologists predict that, by the next century, men and women will live indefinitely long lives, dying mainly from accidents, murder, or war—not from disease or old age. Humans will be like classic automobiles, kept going with spare parts and periodic overhauls. Regular injections of stem cells will revitalize human organs. However, there will still be suffering.

Pain is not an illness, of course, but only a sign of something gone wrong. Unfortunately, pain shouts when a whisper would suffice to motivate us to seek a remedy for the underlying malady. Most of us can be reconciled to chronic conditions, but not to the suffering that accompanies them. So we need to adopt ways of neutralizing the discomfort and even agony that accompanies illness.

Fortunately, because pain is subjective, it can actually be managed through our reaction to it. Unfortunately, many doctors expect their "good" patients not to complain of discomfort, but to grin and bear it. If that is your doctor's attitude, don't buy into it. Everyone is subject to illness from time to time and prone to weaknesses, but no one need be victimized by pain. Fortunately, new drug-delivery systems allow pain-relieving remedies to be absorbed at consistent levels without side effects such as drowsiness and nausea.

Best-selling author Dr. Bernie Siegel reveals that many doctors care inadequately for their own health, so you must prod them to pay full attention to your own well-being. On average, physicians actually have more problems with drugs and alcohol than their patients, as well as a higher suicide rate. And they die sooner after the age of sixty-five.[11] Nonetheless, many doctors hesitate to prescribe narcotics, even to terminally ill patients, for fear that they will create addiction, hasten death, or involve themselves in malpractice suits.

Your pain is aggravated by tension, anxiety, and physical deterioration. By neutralizing those aggravations, suffering is eased, if not completely eliminated. To that end, pain clinics prescribe changes in diet and environment and promote relaxation techniques, exercise programs, and antidepressants. When you are relaxed, fit, and in tolerably good spirits, you can cope with even chronic pain.

CONFRONTING PAIN WITH GUIDED IMAGERY

Everyone's pain is personal. Anyone who says, "I feel your pain," is lying. Because suffering is subjective, we tend to be inarticulate in describing it. As a consequence, physicians have difficulty locating and relieving it. Local anesthetics commonly used for minor operations enjoy only brief effectiveness. Aspirin and other common pain remedies medicate the entire body rather than the site of pain alone and can cause unpleasant side effects. Sometimes the "cure" can be worse than the illness.

Experts in pain control suggest that the first step in relieving pain is to confront it by describing it to ourselves. All pain is not alike. Once you meet your pain and define it, you can be on your way to mastering it. The trick here is to separate yourself from the pain. Instead of complaining that "I hurt," you declare, "The pain is there." Once you localize your pain, you can step back from it and deal with it.

The aim of picturing pain is not to fool yourself, but to insulate yourself from suffering. And it works. As soon as you can picture the pain as tangible, you can ease it from your body by autosuggestion. By picturing warmth, you can bring warmth to your extremities. By relaxation techniques, you can feel the pain seep from your body.

SLEEP

The three pillars of personal health management are sleep, exercise, and nutrition. By rights, sleep should be the easiest of the three to manage, because it literally involves doing nothing but lying flat on your back. But everyone needs sufficient sleep. If you find yourself tired and inattentive during the day, you are probably not getting enough sleep at night. The most effective regimen is to maintain the same hours for retiring and waking every day of the week. "Catching up" on weekends by sleeping late on Sunday or taking the occasional nap will not remedy sleep deprivation.

Dr. James W. Pearce, director of the Sleep Disorders Center of the Pacific in Honolulu, admits that even he misses sleep occasionally and gets a truly refreshing night's rest only on vacation. Here are some of his tips for the rest of the year:

1. Don't oversleep because of the previous night's wakefulness.
2. If you can't sleep, stop trying. Sleep can't be forced.
3. Have a light snack before bedtime.
4. Don't take drugs, including nicotine, alcohol, or caffeine. Even antihistamines before bedtime may have irritating side effects.
5. Practice relaxation techniques, with the help of a prerecorded audiotape if necessary.
6. Don't worry if you don't get eight hours of sleep. You may not need that much rest.
7. Exercise earlier in the day, not just before bedtime.
8. Reserve the bedroom for sleep, not eating, television watching, reading, or working. If sex stimulates you rather than relaxing you, move your love life to a different room and time.
9. If you can't get to sleep until 3 A.M. but must wake at 7, start going to bed at 3 A.M. temporarily. After a week of sleeping well for four hours a night, retire 15 minutes earlier the next night and work your way up incrementally to a full night's sleep.[12]

EXERCISE

Just because exercise is currently fashionable doesn't mean it is popular. Despite Nike's urging the population to "just do it," only one-third of us get much physical activity. You may be a member of the sedentary majority, especially as you get older. Part of the appeal of exercise is that it enhances your feeling of well-being. Nowadays it is also used as part of a regimen to keep weight down and make people feel more attractive. But its real importance is to keep us healthy. Perversely, as our lives become more stressful, we become more inactive physically—a life-shortening combination. Darwin was right about the survival of the fittest.

The benefits of exercise for longevity are proven. The *Journal of the American Medical Association* reports that, for every hour spent exercising, you add two to three hours to your life.[13] The positive effect of physical exercise on your mental health is almost immediate.

The real purpose of exercise is cardiovascular conditioning. The heart, lungs, blood vessels, tendons, and bones are brought to their highest working efficiency. We make better use of oxygen, make the best use of food, and even eliminate body wastes more effectively. To reap these benefits requires endurance (or aerobic) exercise, not just touching your toes or lifting weights. Three 30-minute sessions a week of sustained, moderately vigorous exercise (running or fast walking) is adequate. Loosen up beforehand by stretching so that you won't strain muscles. In aerobic exercise, you break into a sweat. Don't be concerned. That's the sign that it's working.

NUTRITION

The words *nutrition* and *diet* are often used interchangeably, but, increasingly, diet describes weight-loss regimens. Perhaps you need to lose weight to be healthy, but everyone needs good nutrition.

Eating is a pleasure. Arguably, it is the most reliable and democratic pleasure of them all, and the one most open to variety. Sex may be orgasmic, but cuisine can be an art and is a renewable feast. If you doubt me, check any bookstore and count the titles of books that are devoted to food and drink. There are more cookbooks in print than books devoted to pleasing all of our other senses combined.

Food manufacturers now cater to good nutrition with tasty low-salt, low-fat, low-cholesterol, and sugar-free versions of their regular products. But they can't force us to consume them. Treat yourself to good nutrition, and you will live longer while protecting yourself from illness. The late Dr. John Knowles, administrator of Massachusetts General Hospital and president of the Rockefeller Foundation, insisted that "over 99 percent of us are born healthy and are made sick as a result of personal misbehaviors and environmental conditions."[14] You can easily control something as enjoyable as your nutrition.

PREPARE YOUR OWN MEALS

Living on your own, you will be tempted to rely on prepared meals, such as take-outs and TV dinners. And you will be inconsistent about meal times. If you succumb, you will be spending too much for food that falls short of being satisfying and costs much more than you need to pay.

If you can boil water, you can cook for yourself. Even for accomplished chefs, there is less motivation to cook for one than for a family. So consider yourself your family. Get a simple cookbook meant for singles. You will still be preparing more than you can eat in one sitting, so you will have tasty leftovers to enjoy later in the week. When I was living alone, I spent just a few hours, on the weekend, preparing all of the following week's dinners and then slipping them in the freezer. It not only made me look forward to coming home to a home-cooked meal, but it made me feel civilized and in control of my life. I even kept something in reserve in case I had unexpected company. If you are a single parent, preparing the week's meals on the previous weekend means that you won't dread shopping and cooking for the kids every evening.

I hesitate to recommend cookbooks for people who are living alone, but here are two that I found invaluable: Dede Napoli's *The Starving Students' Cookbook* and Pillsbury's *Nice 'n Easy Cookbook*. When I was suddenly single in my early forties (but often cooking for my three daughters), my office coworkers bought me a slow cooker, which was a lifesaver. I could prepare that evening's dinner before I left for work in the morning, turn on the cooker, and a hot meal would be ready to eat when I returned after the workday.

DEALING WITH DOCTORS

My wife and I have a physician who routinely runs late on his appointments. We've learned not to mind his tardiness, because he spends as much time with each patient as that person needs. He treats people, not ailments. Despite disincentives from the HMOs that insure his patients' health care (and provide his living), he routinely refers them to specialists for additional tests, as needed, and he encourages annual physicals, flu shots, exercise, and diet regimens.

I trust that you will find such a doctor, but I must admit that it took many years and much dissatisfaction before we found ours. Despite his professionalism, our physician's practice cannot be very satisfying to him, because he rarely cures anyone but can only prescribe for his patients and counsel them to take better care of themselves. Despite his effort to get people to take charge of their own health management, his waiting room is filled, week after week, with many of the same people, who expect him to work some miracle on bodies that they have abused through the years.

Dr. Salvatore Scialla of Scranton, Pennsylvania, says, "I see my relationship with my patient as a marriage."[15] That's probably too much to ask of your doctor, but it must be a relationship, and a democratic one at that, because you and your physician are jointly responsible for your health.

Just because you are your doctor's patient doesn't mean that patience is the virtue that you bring to that relationship. Physicians have slowly come to acknowledge that the patients whom they consider demanding are the ones who are determined to get and stay well and who do improve. Unfortunately, many doctors are trained to look at their patients and see a disease instead of a person and a life. That is not the kind of doctor you want. To find the right physician, scout around, and set up an interview. If the doctor is too busy for a pretreatment chat, write your candidate a letter and ask how he or she deals long-term with patients.

It is wise to write your doctor in advance of every appointment, reminding him or her of the regimen you are on, the medications you are taking, and the progress you are making. That is the proactive way of presenting yourself and engaging a physician as your collaborator. Your letter will go into your doctor's permanent file and be taken seriously.

Ask a nurse to refer you to the physicians that she recommends in your area. Nurses are conversant about what doctors can and cannot do and how well they deal with patients. Nurses are not bedazzled by medical alchemy. And they, like you, go to doctors when they are ill.

If you don't know any nurses, visit the emergency room of your local hospital and ask a registered nurse to recommend a doctor on the hospital staff who keeps private office hours. You will get a knowledgeable referral. Then tell the doctor the name of the medical professional who recommended him or her to you. Live long and prosper!

RESOURCES

Diet and Eating Disorders

American Anorexia/Bulimia Association 1-212-501-8351

Anorexia Nervosa and Related Eating Disorders, Inc. 1-541-344-1144

Association for the Health Enrichment of Large People 1-703-731-1778

Center for Eating Disorders 1-516-868-6831

Eating Disorders Awareness and Prevention 1-206-382-1587

National Association of Anorexia Nervosa and Associated Disorders 1-847-831-3438

National Center for Overcoming Overeating 1-212-875-0442

Cosmetic Surgery

American Academy of Cosmetic Surgery 1-800-221-9808

American Academy of Facial Plastic and Reconstructive Surgery 1-800-332-FACE

American Board of Medical Specialties 1-800-776-CERT

American Society for Aesthetic Plastic Surgery 1-800-635-0635

American Society of Plastic and Reconstructive Surgeons 1-800-635-0635

American Society for Dermatological Surgery 1-800-441-2737

Let's Face It 1-508-371-3186 (to correct facial disfigurement).

Support Networks

AboutFace USA 1-800-225-FACE

Look Good . . . Feel Better 1-800-395-LOOK

Makeovers

Michael Maron 1-213-4-MAKEUP (He does the Hollywood stars, so he can make you look like one. He also helps burn victims and victims of scarring to look attractive again.)

Alternative Medicine

National Center for Complementary and Alternative Medicine Clearinghouse 1-888-644-6226. This toll-free service of the National Institutes of Health can help you assess the benefits of alternative remedies and lead you to the Center's vast information resources.

Holistic Health Havens 1-702-645-1799

American Foundation for Alternative Health Care, Research and Development 1-914-794-8181

Health Information and Support Groups

The American Wellness Project 1-800-238-6479

American Council for Healthful Living 1-201-674-7476

American Council on Science and Health 1-212-362-7044

American Healthcare Institute 1-202-293-2840

American Health Foundation 1-212-953-1900

Dana Alliance for Brain Initiatives 1-800-65-BRAIN

Foundation for Health 1-315-782-6664

National Health Federation 1-818-357-2181
National Health Information Center 1-301-565-4167
A Wellness Center 1-212-532-4286
Some Websites:
Your Personal Net Doctor www.ypn.com
www.mercer.peachnet.edu/www/health/health.html
www.xnet.com/ hret/statind.htm

Nutrition and Fitness

Here are some Web sites:

www.blonz.com/blonz/index.html
www.ificinfo.health.org
www.dietetics.com
www.worldguide.com/Fitness/hf.html
www.ihr.com

Help with Pain

If you have access to the Internet, use your browser to search the category "pain." Compuserve and America Online have online forums on pain and remedies. Here are some specific Web sites:

www.impaccusa.com
www.tc.cornell.edu/hedge/gradprojects/cheese/BIPP.html
www.alternatives.com/cfs-news/index.htm
www.icdi.wvu.edu/files/file23.htm
International Society for Imagery Science 1-312-240-4040
American Imagery Association 1-619-298-7502
American Pain Society 1-202-296-9200
American Rheumatism Association 1-404-633-3777
International Association for the Study of Pain 1-206-547-6409
National Chronic Pain Outreach Association 1-301-652-4948
National Committee on the Treatment of Intractable Pain 1-202-944-8140
National Headache Foundation 1-312-878-5558
National Head Injury Foundation 1-617-485-9950

Health Care and Insurance

Here are some Web sites:

Food and Drug Administration: www.FDA.gov
CenterWatch (industry-sponsored clinical trials): www.centerwatch.com
National Institutes of Health: http://clinicalstudies.info.nih.gov
Medline, for reports on medical research: www.ncbi.nlm.nih.gov/PubMed/
www.comed.com/amcp
www.hcfa.gov
www.epn.or/idea/health.html
www.amso.com

For the latest information on specific ailments, use your Web browser, typing in the relevant word (e.g., cancer, hypertension, arthritis, prostate). Or have your local research librarian show you how to use the public library's resources, including interactive sites and chat rooms.

Women's Health

Each year, heart attacks kill eleven times as many women as breast cancer. To recognize the symptoms and prevent heart disease, the American College of Obstetricians and Gynecologists offer a free booklet. Call toll-free 1-888-567-0595. Also contact the Society for the Advancement of Women's Health Research: www.womens-health.org.

Aging

Alzheimer's Association 1-800-272-3900
Alzheimer's Disease Education and Referral Center 1-800-438-4380
National Institute on Aging Information Center 1-800-222-2225

Further Reading

Bernie S. Siegel, M.D.
Love, Medicine, and Miracles (Harper & Row, 1986)
Peace, Love, and Healing (Harper & Row, 1989)
How to Live Between Office Visits (HarperCollins, 1993)

Pay Your Bills and Reward Yourself

People who tell you money can't buy happiness don't know where to shop.

Anonymous

Living on your own at any stage in your life entails paying your own bills. If you have dependents, it means paying theirs as well. The advantage that you enjoy by being on your own is that you alone have the freedom to choose how you spend and save your money for your greatest satisfaction. Do I hear you complain that many of your outlays are not of your choosing at all but are imposed on you?

Granted, you need to pay for a roof over your head, food to sustain you, a way of getting around, and utilities. Still, you control where you choose to live, what you eat, and the size of your phone and heating bills, as well as the age and economy of the car you drive. Henry David Thoreau, the famed hermit of Walden Pond, who single-handedly built his cabin in the Massachusetts woods with a borrowed axe, would not sympathize with such complaints. His counsel was the following: make friends with yourself and simplify your life, which will shrink your budget. You can do that at any stage in your life. But, to succeed, you have to control your consumerism.

GETTING AHEAD FINANCIALLY

Barely 15 minutes from my home is one of the largest discount shopping malls in the United States. Potomac Mills is the number-one tourist attraction in the entire state of Virginia, overshadowing Mount Vernon, home of our first president. Every day, the mall's gargantuan parking lots are filled with automobiles and tour buses. Ranking with the Capitol and the White House, Potomac Mills is also a magnet for the millions of foreign visitors to the nation's capital every year. Who can blame them? How can anyone pass up a chance to buy Limoges china or a Ralph Lauren suit at just half the retail price? The answer, of course, is anyone who doesn't really need them. Nothing is a bargain if you can't afford it, and, even if you can, there are other options for spending your money. You can even save it to spend later. But shop-till-you-drop has become America's favorite pastime, with the result that we have been transformed from citizens into a nation of consumers.

The fallout from this phenomenon has been dreadful. Every year, more Americans file for bankruptcy than graduate from college.[1] Rest assured, the bankrupt are not all poor people. Many are middle-class Americans with steady jobs who are simply spending way beyond their means. Stand in a checkout line and note how many people pay by check, using a credit card only for identification. Naïvely, I once asked a clerk why anyone would use a credit card in such a strange way. Because they've exceeded their credit limit, I was told; their card is no longer good for anything except as identification.

In dire cases, bankruptcy is a sensible and welcome option. At the very least, it allows you to consolidate your debts and pay them off slowly so that you don't starve and won't be bothered by creditors. At best, all of your debts will be forgiven and you can start afresh. Either way, however, your credit rating suffers for a time, so it's better to discipline your spending now rather than have the courts and credit agencies do it later.

It was only after my remarriage at age forty-four that I emerged permanently from debt. Before then, it was an exercise in juggling bills against short-term loans, hoping each month that my paycheck would clear in time to cover the check to my landlord. But getting out of debt proved to be much more than mere convenience. The full force of financial wisdom finally hit me: when you're in debt, you pay others interest on your plight. On the other hand, when you have savings, others pay you for the use of your money. The choice is to be a financial winner or a loser. Living on your own, you cannot afford to be a loser.

The average American is burdened with $7,200 in revolving debt (mostly on credit cards), and $21,000 in total debt. Meanwhile, on average, those of us who do save squirrel away just one penny of every two dollars remaining after essential living expenses.[2]

That explains our nation's anxiety about preserving Social Security. In addition to a monthly check from the government, your own parents probably also count on retirement income from pensions. But pensions have long since been replaced by IRAs and 401K plans, which place the burden of saving for the future on you rather than on your employer. Fewer than half of Americans approaching retirement have saved anything toward their later years. Many count on the equity in their homes to finance retirement. But the Center for Housing Policy estimates that, today, an income of nearly $85,000 is needed to afford a medium-priced house in the first instance. That assumes a 10 percent down payment, plus 28 percent of your income for mortgage, taxes, and insurance.[3]

The problem is that a house is not a liquid asset. You can't sell it and still live in it. More and more, we see senior citizens taking part-time minimum wage jobs just to put food on the table while they live in homes that they've already paid for. I'm embarrassed to see men and women past retirement age toil in the heat and cold, loading groceries into supermarket customers' station wagons. Believe me, they're not still working just to "keep busy."

If you're younger and on your own, it's likely that you are still renting an apartment and enriching your landlord, instead of building equity for yourself. Consider this: single women living alone account for more than one-fifth of all of the homes sold in America. Investment adviser Vanessa Summers notes that, at any time, 10 percent of all homes in America are for sale—including condo apartments and townhouses, as well as stand-alone houses. If you expect to live on your own in the same area for an indefinite period, consider building up equity by buying a place of your own. Maybe you can't afford your dream home at first, but you should build equity so that you can trade up.[4]

If you're living on a fixed income in your later years and already own a home, you can obtain a reverse mortgage to increase your monthly income, while you shop for an assisted living facility where others do the cleaning, prepare your meals, and see to your health.

THE ILLUSION OF AFFLUENCE

It's the appearance of affluence across America that prompts us to spend. It's what used to be called "keeping up with the Joneses." Contrary to appearances, we actually have less discretionary income than we did a generation ago. Despite two incomes, the median married couple gained little ground in the past twenty years, and the earnings of the bottom one-fifth of wage earners has actually lost purchasing power.

If married couples with two incomes are struggling financially, it's usually because they have children to raise, but it is also because they have increased their expectations of the good life. Living on your own, with but one income, you have only one person to satisfy—yourself—and can tame or defer your expectations without complaints from others who feel short-changed.

While real incomes have stalled or shrunk, real prices have risen. Because of the example of others, Americans have gone on a spending spree, raising everyone's ante. Because of rising expectations, married couples spend more than ever at Christmas and on birthdays; they buy sneakers for their growing kids that cost more than their own dress shoes and send their sons and daughters to colleges and universities that they would never have considered for themselves because they knew they couldn't afford them. As a person living on your own, consider this: even if you could afford them, you still couldn't have everything. Where would you put it all?

Lest you suspect Americans are only buying more but paying less for it, consider that the floor space of the average new home being built (and mortgaged!) today is more than double what it was in the 1970s. The average price of a new car has ballooned more than 75 percent in the past decade.[5]

Not only are Americans spending more; we're demanding luxuries. Financial adviser Andrew Tobias warns, "A luxury once sampled becomes a necessity. Pace yourself!" For example, can you recall exactly when you started thinking that a cup of coffee was worth five dollars rather than twenty-five cents? The Starbucks empire was built on that sea change in perceptions. Consider this: sales of quality wines have soared by 23 percent every year since 1980. Sales of wristwatches costing $2,000 or more rose 13 percent in a recent year alone. One of every eight new vehicles on the road is now a luxury automobile or an SUV. A decade ago, it was only one in fifteen.[6]

Oscar Wilde famously defined a cynic as one "who knows the price of everything and the value of nothing." His aphorism would have to be revised today, because no one knows the price of anything until he or she checks the sales. But Wilde was correct about assessing value—not just the quality of the goods that we buy and the pleasures that we purchase—but the actual value that they add to our lives.

One of the advantages of living on your own is that no one else can impose his or her values on you. Once you decide what you need—versus what you only fantasize about—you will know what measures to take regarding money. And you will be as rich as Rockefeller in life satisfaction. But if you're poor as a church mouse at the moment, it's time to get rid of the red ink in your budget.

How and where you obtain your money is another subject altogether. But what you do with your money is within your control. Consider the alternatives that you enjoy by living on your own and the opportunities you have to secure your life financially.

CHOICES THAT YOU CAN MAKE NOW

1. You can start saving. Saving, like spending, is simply a habit. Breathing is a habit too; if we had to think before taking each breath, we'd have little attention left for anything else. Fortunately, a good habit is no harder to develop than a bad one. Saving and spending are not antagonistic. You are only saving now to spend later on something better.

2. You can reduce expenses. But it's not easy. Cutting down is infinitely harder than cutting out. For example, let's say you spend $300 a month at the supermarket, mostly for food and household products. Reducing that expense means settling for cheaper products or depriving yourself of things that you like. You will feel poor. You can't reduce your water bill, heating, or electric bill without discomfort either. So look to other parts of your budget; then eliminate those expenses altogether. The easiest expenses to jettison are those associated with your workday or time away from home. Instead of eating lunch out and drinking those $2 cups of coffee on the run, pack your lunch and carry a thermos. Professional clothing is expensive and uncomfortable. Accessorize the wardrobe you already have, saving instead for comfortable clothes that you can wear at home and at leisure. Fire your cleaning lady and tidy up your house or apartment yourself. Who knows? You may just develop the habit of keeping it clean. Don't buy books or magazines that you can get free from the library. Sell that second car, which you seldom drive, along with anything else that you have but don't use regularly. It's a simple formula: Don't skimp. Eliminate.

3. You can live on a budget. Budgeting simply means knowing where your money is going so that you can be sure to have enough of it when you need it. The Internal Revenue Service requires you to fill out forms each year to demonstrate how much you owe your government. It's even easier to construct a personal or household budget that shows you how much you owe yourself. Just keep track of your expenses, by category, for three months, and don't forget to factor in those big annual and semiannual bills, such as auto insurance, vacations, and Christmas gifts. Once you determine, on average, how much you spend each month in each expense category, keep track in subsequent months to see whether you've gone over your limit. Even celebrities learn to live on budgets. Twin actresses Ashley and Mary-Kate Olsen were worth millions even before they reached their teens, but they each received just $7 a week as an allowance. If they skipped a household chore, they got a dollar deducted. As a boy, President John F. Kennedy received fifty cents in allowance per week; the Rockefeller brothers got just twenty-five cents each.

4. But beware of cash. It's practically impossible to budget when you spend cash. Of course, you could always save all of your sales slips, but you won't. Instead,

use checks and credit cards, which provide a handy, automatic record of what you are spending—and on what. Credit cards are best because they defer your payments. Debit cards are less attractive, because they require you to know exactly how much is in your checking account. You can even get discounts or frequent flier miles by using your cards. I get a free trip to Europe every year for using one of mine for every possible expense. Choose a card that has no annual fee and pay off the balance in full every month. Don't carry a checkbook, but keep a desk-sized checkbook and write checks only at home, keeping a running balance so that you don't overdraw.

5. You can save regularly. Make savings an integral item in your budget, preferably the same amount every month. It may be one of the smaller categories, but it should be at the very top of the budget. It's not what you owe others, but what you owe yourself. Pay it first.

6. You can set aside money for predictable expenses. If you have a car, you will need to replace it sometime, so prepare for that eventuality now. Otherwise, when the time comes, you will feel constrained to buy a new model and pay for it on time with interest. By setting something aside now, you can build up a fund and, when the time comes, pay cash for an almost-new car that costs half the dealer's tariff. Plan for emergencies. In a recent year, practically everything mechanical in our lives died and needed replacing: the dishwasher, refrigerator, VCR, iron, vacuum cleaner, and two televisions. Moreover, the car needed expensive repairs, and the kitchen flooded and needed a new floor. Worst of all, the furnace failed in midwinter and needed replacing, followed by the heat pump. To boot, I needed expensive dental work. Those were all emergencies, but, frankly, every one was predictable. I just didn't know that they would all happen at the same time. They did not bust our budget or turn us suicidal, because we had set aside savings for the worst. You can too. When I turned sixty-five, I took out an insurance policy to cover catastrophic illness and nursing home care. That was an unwelcome addition to an already tight budget, but it relieves my mind and ensures that my wife will not be left with me as an expensive dependent.

7. You can increase your income. But, rest assured, this is not a remedy for overspending. Unless you establish a budget and control it, you will spend every extra dollar that you earn—and more. America's consumer debt stands at 13.4 percent of disposable income.[7] That means we're spending $1.13 for every dollar that we earn—no matter how many dollars are in the paycheck. The only solution is to spend less.

BORROWING

Once you have some regular savings, no matter how small, you will be able to invest, and your wealth will multiply geometrically, because everyone will want to pay you for the use of your money. We'll consider some smart alternatives a few pages along. But if you're so deeply in debt now that savings are out of the question, your opportunity to start over begins with a rescue mission.

Incidentally, if you think that almost everyone owes money on their credit cards, you're mistaken. Forty-two percent of credit card holders pay off their balances in full every month.[8] The cards are simply a convenience to them, as they should be, not a floating loan at high interest.

Everyone has to borrow money sometime (even millionaires have mortgages), but you don't have to go broke borrowing. When the U.S. Treasury is prepared to pay you less than 5 percent for the use of your money, why should you pay VISA or MasterCard three times as much for the use of theirs?

One of your best ploys for starting over financially is to join a credit union, which is probably the best source of unsecured loans at low interest. Joining a credit union is wise in any case, because you can't borrow unless you also have a savings account there, so it supports your saving habit. If there's no credit union at your place of business, find one through an organization that you belong to. A credit union is like a volunteer fire department. Just as no one should make a profit putting out fires, no one needs to make a killing lending you money.

Another source of cheap money is your life insurance policy. You can borrow on your insurance as long as you have a whole-life policy rather than simple term. If you own your own home or apartment, you've already borrowed much of its value by taking out a mortgage. But, with a home equity loan, you can borrow against the portion of your dwelling's value that is already yours. For example, if it's worth $150,000 and your mortgage balance is $100,000, you have $50,000 worth of equity with which to secure a loan from a bank.

Banks compete to lend you this money cheaply because they can't lose (they'll take your home or apartment if you default). They're not doing you a favor, so you don't have to beg. It couldn't be easier. You're given a line of credit indicating your borrowing limit, plus a checkbook. You simply write checks to yourself or your creditors and repay a small portion of your balance each month. Best of all, the interest on these loans is tax-deductible. Becky and I used our home equity account to help pay for our daughters' college tuition. Now the account is still there should we have an emergency and don't want to touch retirement savings that are in investments, earning much more.

CREDIT

If you are refused credit, you must discover why. Check your local Yellow Pages under "Credit Reporting Agencies" and write each of them requesting a copy of your report. In your request, include your full name, Social Security number, current and former addresses, and the name of your spouse. Enclose a copy of the letter from the merchant who denied you credit. By law, the agency must supply your report to you, explain your credit rating, and correct any errors contained in your record.

I send for my report routinely every year, because every one has errors. I am now nearly thirty years into a second marriage, but the agencies continued for years to recognize only my first spouse. You have the right to dispute your rating in person. You can also add information to your file that may help explain any late payments or disputes with creditors.

If you ever get turned down for a loan or mortgage, you have the right to know why. Write the lender within ten days. By law, lenders must explain their decisions. That allows you to provide them with better information or to approach another lender with a stronger case. If any creditor refuses to file correct information on you to the credit bureau, take that merchant to your local small claims court. For a small fee and no need for an attorney, you will get compliance. Creditors hate going to court, so they'll likely comply immediately after your threat.

Financial adviser Jane Bryant Quinn suggests that you may be in financial trouble if your monthly debt payments exceed 20 percent of your monthly income.[9] If that's the case, don't wait until your credit is denied altogether to get help. Fortunately, there is plenty of assistance to go around. Debt counseling service is a competitive field, and it's financed not by debtors, but by creditors. That's right: the people to whom you owe money pay anywhere from 6 to 12 percent to professional advisers to help you reorganize your finances in order to continue to make the payments that you owe. Why do creditors become so generous when the chips are down? Because the alternative is that you will choose bankruptcy and they will collect nothing at all, or nothing for a long time.

A counseling service analyzes your income and expenses, helps you make payments, and tells you how to stay out of debt in the future. If your finances are utterly out of control, your counselor will devise a formal debt repayment plan, take a single monthly payment from you, and distribute a portion to each of your creditors. The result is that those creditors instantly stop hounding you. Many may even lower your monthly payment and interest rate or waive late payment fees altogether until you've caught up. But be aware: you won't be able to run up any more charges on those accounts until you're clear.

On average, it could take between four and six years to pay off your current debts through a counseling service. But you will still be able to put food on the table and avoid bankruptcy and harassment while maintaining your self-respect.

BANKRUPTCY

You probably associate workhouses with the novels of Charles Dickens, but, as a child growing up in Depression-era Chicago, I remember my parents driving past a grim Cook County institution they called the "poor house." It was the twentieth-century version of a debtors' prison.

At some point, society decided that it was pointless to incarcerate people simply because they couldn't pay their bills (obviously they couldn't pay them any better from prison). Bankruptcy laws were passed because Congress acknowledged that it was better to give people a second chance to pay their way through life than to condemn them to penury. To file for Chapter 7 bankruptcy, you need a lawyer (see the Yellow Pages for specialists, preferably those who offer a free initial consultation). Once a judge discharges your debts, you are no longer responsible for paying them. No creditor can even attempt to make you repay. You cannot be harassed—ever.

However, depending on the court's judgment, you may still be responsible for "nondischargeable debts," including alimony, student loans, and tax obligations. But your assets will not be wiped out. Most states allow bankrupts to keep the equity in their homes, their automobile, and their personal property.

Once the court relieves you of your debts, you have only those assets. If you are employed, your wages have to sustain you, because no bank will lend you money and no merchant will extend credit to you. Should you change jobs, any prospective employer could request your credit report and learn of your situation. However, that's an unlikely event, so you can look for a better paying job that improves your finances.

As soon as possible, you want to restore your credit and get ahead of the game. First, correct everything in your credit reports that is false or misleading. Send corrections by certified mail, with a return receipt requested. If need be, you can later prove that the bureaus received your request. Unless corrected, bad credit information remains in your file for seven years. By law, bankruptcy stays on your record for ten years.

If you have steady income and don't want to place yourself in the hands of a credit counselor, choosing Chapter 13 bankruptcy can restore your credit in three years. Unlike Chapter 7 applications, Chapter 13 bankruptcies still require you to pay your creditors most of what you owe them, but only over an extended time, during which they cannot harass you. You need a judge's approval to stretch out payments, but you won't need to pay a lawyer to make your case for you.

If Chapter 13 is your choice, experts advise that you allocate no more than 25 percent of your income to debt repayment. You must list all debts with the court and show that you can pay them off in about three years. When your application is approved, you make a single payment from each paycheck to the court, which then disburses the money to your creditors. They cannot bother you or charge you additional interest for the extended repayment period.

In April 2005, Congress passed, and the president signed, a law restricting those who could file for complete dismissal of their debts (Chapter 7) to persons with incomes at the median or less in their state of residence. If you earn more than the average citizen of your state, you must file for Chapter 13 instead. Moreover, the new law requires that anyone filing for bankruptcy pay for credit counseling.

TO REESTABLISH CREDIT

If you want to remove your bad credit ratings sooner than ten years after Chapter 7, experts recommend that you write to each creditor and strike a bargain. For example, if you owed $1,000 to a furniture company before having that debt discharged by the court, consider offering the store $200 on the understanding (in writing) that the merchant will remove the bad debt notice altogether from your report. That's not bribery, just a good bargain all around. The furniture store gets $200 (instead of nothing) and you get a chance to start over with a good credit rating.

If you have many creditors and little cash, that course may not be feasible. In that case, disregard your bad credit report and start establishing a good one:

1. Establish a savings account in a bank or credit union and make small but regular contributions to it.
2. Then go to a loan officer in the same institution and ask to borrow an amount equal to your savings on the understanding that your loan will be secured by your savings account. Make sure that the loan is reported to the credit bureau.
3. Then take the borrowed money and open a savings account in another bank, making it collateral for another loan there. Now you have two savings accounts. Of course, you're paying interest on your two loans, but your regular payments prove that you're trustworthy. You're rebuilding credit.
4. Apply for a VISA or MasterCard, using one of your savings accounts as collateral. Often, a bank will offer you a credit line of 150 percent of your savings balance. With a $1,000 passbook savings account, you have a credit card with

a $1,500 spending limit. But here's a warning: apply for these cards directly, not through a middleman.

5. Resume use of any accounts that you did not include in your bankruptcy application—those that had a zero balance when you filed for protection. There is no reason why these former creditors would know, or think to ask, about your financial condition. As far as they're concerned, you've always been solvent.

6. Now, keep up with your payments. Practically speaking, you're solvent.

But here's another warning: many Americans emerging from Chapter 7 bankruptcy find their mailboxes filled with offers of new "preapproved" credit cards, which can appear to be manna from heaven. The credit card companies actually target bankrupts with these offers, knowing that any unpaid balances run up on the new cards do not have bankruptcy protection but must be paid in full with accumulated interest. These cards can charge upward of 15 percent interest on unpaid balances. To default on such cards could mean jail time.

CO-SIGNING

When I first married, credit cards weren't common. I had no debts, but no savings and no credit either. Still, I needed a car. Fortunately, I had a steady job, so my father-in-law co-signed my auto loan. Clearly, he took a risk that I wouldn't keep up payments (then he'd be liable for the balance due), but he had already entrusted his daughter to me. And it didn't cost him anything.

As you are surely aware, however, families break up over money, so it may be better to ask a friend rather than a relative to co-sign with you on a loan. If you don't have a co-signer, you can still probably purchase a car on credit, but your required down payment will be larger. So, too, will be the interest on your loan.

What about a new start on housing while you're still under the cloud of bankruptcy? Assuming that you can afford the payments, you can still rent a house or apartment if you explain your situation to the landlord before he or she sees your credit report. Then offer a larger than usual security deposit. That's free money to any landlord, and landlords can evict you before they are out of pocket on your rent.

If you are in the market to buy a house or condo, start with the bank where you've established a savings account and taken out a loan. If the loan officer still rates you as too great a risk, try your credit union. Credit unions tend to be more liberal with auto loans and can be understanding about home loans as well. At worst, you'll be required to provide a larger than usual down payment and to pay somewhat higher interest. But, after a few payments, your credit will be restored, and later you can refinance at a lower rate.

You can apply for a Federal Housing Authority (FHA) mortgage loan within just one year after your bankruptcy discharge; you need only a modest down payment, and you can enjoy market interest rates. If you are a veteran, you can apply for a mortgage with no money down. If you're not a veteran, you can still assume an existing Veterans Administration loan on the home that you want.

INVESTING

Once you start saving, you have joined the ranks of investors. That's unless you're like my late mother-in-law, who kept gold Krugerrands under the bedroom floorboards, fearing that America was going the way of the Weimar Republic, when a loaf of bread cost a wheelbarrow full of Deutschmarks. Her savings were safe, to be sure, but they didn't earn anything.

Popular financial adviser Andrew Tobias provides a handy formula for taking charge of your finances and making your money multiply:

 Make a budget, scrimp and save, quit smoking, fully fund your retirement plan and start early—tomorrow, if you possibly can—putting away $100 or $500 or $5,000 a month, whatever you can comfortably afford, in two places: short- and intermediate-term Treasury securities, for money you may need in a few years; into no-load, low-expense stock market "index funds," both U.S. and foreign, for everything else. You will do better than 80% of your friends and neighbors.[10]

If you're under the age of fifty, experts suggest that you put 80 percent of savings into stock funds, 20 percent in bonds. As you approach retirement, move more into bonds for stability. Remember that you are not saving for a rainy day. Rather, you are investing in sunlight for the rest of your life.

If you find investing boring, you're like most people, including me. Happily, we don't have to do the work. The nation's mutual fund companies do it all. Basically, they pool the savings of millions of Americans and invest for you, charging only a small service fee that you will never miss. You deal with the funds entirely over the phone (they don't even put you on "hold") and by mail. They regularly inform you about how your money is doing. (If you're anxious, of course, you can check the newspaper every day.)

Mutual funds are for people who don't intend to play the market, but only want to ensure a solvent future. Incidentally, your mutual fund savings aren't inaccessible. Just a phone call returns them to you for any reason whatsoever. If your savings are in tax-deferred funds such as IRAs and 401(k)s, you pay a penalty for early withdrawal.

A little consistent saving can make you a millionaire. Don't take my word for it. The magic is in compound interest. Say you're earning $35,000 and you put 4 percent of that in your employer's 401(k) retirement plan. That's just $27 each week out of your paycheck (it's less if you figure the taxes that would be assessed if you pocketed that $27). What's $27? The price of a book you could borrow instead, free, from the library. Assuming a modest 7 percent rate of return on your savings, you will have $590,134.11 in fifty years—or well over a million dollars if your employer matches your contributions. You may actually have much more, because, over the long run, stocks perform at a rate that is better than 7 percent.

To find mutual funds that appeal to you, consult the annual issues of *Money* and *Kiplingers* magazines, which list the performance of all funds. You'll see how much given funds have returned over the past year, five years, and ten years. Despite some big winners, most funds don't perform as well as the market as a whole, so follow Andrew Tobias's advice and invest in "market index" funds, which make investments that mimic the overall market.

SPENDING

Living on your own, you can set spending priorities that satisfy your goals, not anyone else's. In a recent year, pet care was the fourth largest expense in our budget (after food, housing, and health expenses) because of our dog's and cats' serious health problems. We didn't mind. They're precious to us.

Sometimes the cheapest products are the best ones, because they are less complicated. Our new heating and air conditioning system is only the budget model, admittedly less efficient than top-of-the line units. But *Consumer Reports* warns that the more expensive systems require more servicing at extra cost.

In my book *Spiritual Simplicity*, I suggested easy strategies for saving time and money and even a few ways of making extra money. I won't repeat them here except to warn that any sensible budget and savings plan founders if you allow big expenses to overwhelm you. Divorce, catastrophic illness, college expenses, and major repair bills can spoil your success in living on your own.

Fortunately, you can purchase insurance for life, health, disability, and catastrophic illness. You can even buy insurance that pays your mortgage if you lose your job. But beware: some policies are rip-offs, and some are simply not worth the premiums. For example, purchase cheap term-life insurance rather than whole-life policies. The money that you save can be invested during your lifetime. Any money that you intend to leave to survivors will still be fully protected in the event of your death. If you don't have anyone obvious to leave money to, skip life insurance altogether.

If you're a single parent, your children's college expenses are predictable and manageable. We knew that we would have three daughters in college at the same time. To keep tuition and living expenses within reason, they attended community college while living at home and then transferred to tax-supported state colleges. The exception was our middle daughter, who transferred to the private (and expensive) Corcoran School of Art across from the White House. When she ran out of money after her junior year, she agreed to drop out and work for a year to save for senior-year expenses. As a result, our daughters received college degrees all around and there were no lingering debts for them or us.

Before you go into debt paying for prestigious college degrees, remember that employers seldom if ever ask where their applicants went to college or even what their grades were but only whether they graduated.

SPENDING ON OTHERS

Andrew Tobias tells us what Ebenezer Scrooge learned the hard way: that there's a difference between being frugal and being cheap. The former is a virtue, the latter a vice. Generally, we are frugal with ourselves, shopping for quality and discounts. But we can be cheap with other people, leaving a 10 percent tip for good service instead of 15 or 20 percent. It's not wise to save at the expense of other people.

When you're living on your own, one item in your budget should be devoted to saving the world, or at least a small part of it. It's up to you how you do it—through church or charities—but you must give something back as a sign of gratitude for what you have been given. It's not really expensive to be generous. When David Baldacci made a fortune from his first novel, he considered it unexpected good fortune and shared most of his royalties with his family and friends. With his second novel, he became wealthy himself.

Ironically, the poorest one-fifth of Americans actually contribute a larger percentage of their after-tax income to charity than Americans who earn $100,000 or more.[11] Maybe that's because they know better what it's like to go without. Of course, wealthy people itemize their donations and get tax deductions. Still, on average, they contribute less than 3 percent of their income to making the world a better place. You can appreciate firsthand what it's like to live on your own. So you're primed to appreciate what it's like for those less fortunate.

GET ADVICE

There's wisdom in the cliché that one must sometimes spend money to make money. That's not an invitation to play the lottery, but only a suggestion that you occasionally pay an expert for a little advice. If you are like most Americans, you already seek assistance with your income tax returns, but you may use a commercial tax preparer who learned the basics in a brief course and works only at filing time. Even certified public accountants (CPA) are too overworked at tax time to help you with your overall financial planning.

Here's a warning: don't ask anyone for advice who wants to sell you something. Some stockbrokers and insurance agents offer "free" financial planning that is biased. When my wife and I were approaching retirement, we went to a neighborhood CPA who had nothing to gain from her counseling but a $75 fee. For that, she told us everything that we needed to do to protect our investments, reduce our taxes, and provide insurance against future disability. We've followed through on every one of her strategies. They ensure that we don't have to worry about a time when one of us must make it on his or her own.

RESOURCES

Commercials for MasterCard proclaim: "Some things are priceless; for everything else there's MasterCard." But there are also things that are absolutely free, such as help with your finances. Start with any personal finance book, available at your public library. Pass by any book that pretends to have secrets about how to make a killing. If someone writes a book about them, they aren't secrets any longer.

Here are some other resources:

Mutual Funds. Look at *Money* or *Kiplinger's* magazines for a complete listing, noting performance and toll-free phone numbers. As for U.S. Treasuries, they can be purchased through any bank or broker. Or contact any Federal Reserve branch.

Debt Counseling Services. Here are three reputable ones:

Consumer Credit Counseling Service. 1-800-388-2227 or www.nfcc.org. There are 1,500 offices nationwide. Most offer free counseling. For debt-repayment planning, they ask for $5 to $25 per month contribution, but it's not necessary.

Debt Counselors of America. 1-800-680-3328 or www.getoutofdebt.org. Counseling is free. Debt-repayments planning costs a voluntary $2.90 per creditor per month. "Crisis relief" to forestall imminent bankruptcy costs $299, which includes the services of staff lawyers.

Genus Credit Management. 1-888-436-8715 or www.genus.org. Sells monthly repayment plans by phone, dealing with unsecured debts of over $2,000. Voluntary fee is $3 per month per creditor.

Banks Offering Secured Credit Cards

Ask your own bank first.

Credit Bureaus

Look first in your local directory under "Credit Reporting Services." If there is no listing, use these toll-free numbers:

Equifax 1-800-685-1111
Trans Union 1-800-888-4213
TRW 1-800-392-1122

Other Useful Resources

Credit Union National Association 1-800-358-5710 (for referrals to credit unions near you)

Quotesmith Corporation 1-800-556-9393 (offers quotes for lowest term-life insurance)

Bank Rate Monitor 1-407-627-7330 (provides information on low-interest-rate credit cards)

Internal Revenue Service 1-800-829-3676 (request the guide to free tax services)

10

Enjoy Yourself
(It's Later than You Think)

The most delicious pleasure is to cause that of other people.

La Bruyère

By anyone's standards, the life of Tara Palmer-Tomkinson is exhausting, and it shows. The professional partygoer, now in her late thirties, is fashionably pencil-thin. Having a good time, she confides, can be hard work, especially during the years when she was expected to reveal each week's revelry in a column for London's *Sunday Times*. American party girl Paris Hilton, a decade younger, agrees. "I work my ass off," she confides.

Because fun can be exhausting, Tara found herself, on the cusp of the millennium, recuperating at the Meadows, a rest spa in Arizona, until she could once again charge the trenches of café society. The pursuit of gaiety often required her to attend three parties a night and to make nonstop small talk to bores. Formal dinners were worse. On one occasion, she reveals, "I sat next to a broker who talked about junk bonds all night. I told him the only bonds I knew were Sean Connery and Pierce Brosnan."

Tara has bemoaned her single status but noted with relish to her editor that the clinic in which she was resting also deals with sex addicts. "You might never see me again," she teased.[1]

Although many mortals concur on the pursuit of happiness as a goal in life, few of us confuse ultimate contentment with mere pleasure-seeking. It is children, not adults, who are wont to complain, "Are we having fun yet?" After awhile, like Tara, most adults, single or married, are too tired for a constant round of revelry and the inevitable letdown of the morning after.

Yet social scientists and seers alike identify happiness with activity. Bliss, they insist, is not some pot of gold at the end of the rainbow, but the adventure of riding the rainbow itself wherever it takes us.

Lottery winners, who strike it rich, typically make the mistake of assuming that happiness can be purchased—that it consists of equal parts of leisure and consumption. Accordingly, they quit their employment and desert their communities to become full-time consumers. Later, most admit that they were more content before their financial windfall, just making a living, enjoying family and neighbors, and pursuing the simple pleasures that they could afford.

As a single seeking a more fulfilling life, you may have to break ingrained habits that have denied you many innocent pleasures that are your birthright. Be vigilant: the effective pursuit of happiness demands your attention and personal investment. You may have to set limits on those closest to you who have a stake in keeping you emotionally and financially tied to them. It's easy for people to pick on singles, assuming that you have no life of your own apart from them. Don't fall for the abuse. All of us sacrifice for those we love, but when self-sacrifice becomes a way of life thrust on us by our loved ones, it becomes dysfunctional.

BUSINESS OR PLEASURE?

International travelers are challenged by customs officers with the question, "Are you here for business or pleasure?" Don't hesitate to answer: "Pleasure." The business side of life will turn you into a responsible robot if you let it, but your enjoyment of life is a sign of gratitude for its gift.

Anthropologist Lionel Tiger asks rhetorically, "What is wrong with hedonism, so long as people turn up for work on time, obey traffic signals, recycle beer cans, and do not abuse the welfare and dignity of others?"[2] Typically, those men and women who enjoy life to the full are not only responsible but give of themselves to others, adding to the common good.

Dr. David G. Myers is a psychologist who has devoted his life to dissecting the traits that happy people share. Here is his list:

Fit and healthy bodies

Realistic goals and expectations

Positive self-esteem

Feelings of control

Optimism

Outgoingness

Supportive friendships that enable companionship and confidences

Challenging work and active leisure, punctuated by adequate rest and retreat

A personal faith that entails communal support, purpose, acceptance, outward focus, and hope.[3]

Notice that none of these happy traits comes in a gift package, nor can they be purchased. But they can all be achieved by singles of all ages and conditions. Each addition offers you the opportunity to create more enjoyment in your life.

Psychologists agree that if you start acting "as if" you are happy, you will find that contentment becomes a habit as easily acquired as any other. Granted, pleasure-seeking can be abused, but only if we are frivolous in our enjoyments or too demanding of our senses. Excessive indulgence of taste can lead to gluttony, just as a frantic sex life can lead to promiscuity. By contrast, connoisseurs of fine wine do not overindulge their passion, nor does a faithful lover regard his or her beloved as a mere sex object for personal consumption.

The English philosopher Jeremy Bentham observed that "nature has placed mankind under the governance of two sovereign masters, pain and pleasure. It is for them alone to point out what we ought to do, as well as to determine what we shall do."[4]

Because the majority of men and women worldwide are impoverished, they give priority to safety and the avoidance of pain. But, even in affluent America, our Puritan heritage can incline us to believe that we are moral when we are only uncomfortable, suspecting that it is bad to feel good. Needless to say, life and love continue to make demands on us, but their rewards surpass their trials. Instead, seek enjoyment in life in full confidence that you will give joy to others as well. Enjoyment is the highest form of gratitude for the gift of life.

THE TYRANNY OF TIME

Are you too busy to enjoy yourself? Many Americans believe that they are. Perversely, the first things that they slight are the activities and relationships that most please them. Workaholics employ time-management strategies to squeeze more labor into fewer hours, rather than to apply those efficiencies to yield leisure and enjoyment.

The acronym GNP stands for "gross national product" rather than "gross national pleasure." That's a shame. The poet Stephen Spender lamented that Americans "are better at having a love affair that lasts 10 minutes than any other people in the world."[5]

As a single, you can vouch for the fact that romance has surely suffered from "busy-ness." Once, couples took time for courtship, flowers, and love letters, but they now head straight for the mattress, turning sex into a spasm instead of the abiding pleasure that it is meant to be. Although sex sells fiction, few novels depict happy married relationships.

The American fascination with retirement stems from the belief that retirees finally have the time to enjoy the earnings of a life devoted to labor. But when they reach their mid-sixties, many Americans discover that they are out of practice, having never developed the habit of pleasing themselves. In an earlier book, *Spiritual Simplicity*, I suggested how busy people can slow down and reduce the burdens that impede their enjoyment. Simpler living affords ample time to pursue happiness more effectively.

Enjoyment is a habit that comes naturally to those who free themselves to recognize the truth, beauty, and goodness around them, whereas the preoccupied and absentminded alike miss the good life. If you doubt me, consider that, in Great Britain alone, men lose the equivalent of $1.6 million in paper currency every day because they launder their trousers without checking their pockets first for cash. That's literally money down the drain because of inattention. At the same time, only a minority of Britons equip their homes with showers, wisely preferring leisurely and sybaritic baths. A shower is swifter, more efficient, and uses less water, but to soak in a hot tub has been an enjoyment since Roman times. Like all pleasures, it must be savored, and that takes time.

To be sure, the ability to postpone gratification is the sign of a civilized man or woman. And excess is the enemy of contentment. But to deny pleasure altogether or to be indifferent to enjoyment are marks of ingratitude for the gift of life. As a single, you are in sole charge of your happiness.

THE PRICE OF PLEASURE

It is always possible to live beneath your financial means, but few Americans do. Singles and marrieds alike look at their credit card statements and wonder why they are in debt when they derived so little enjoyment from their expenditures. As you embrace your single life, consider your priorities. Are you are actually overspending on necessities when you could be devoting a larger portion of your dollars and time to enjoying a few luxuries?

Of course, everyone's idea of what constitutes a luxury is different. But some luxuries are affordable. At New York's Four Seasons Hotel, the same bottle of Evian water costs $10 from room service but only $1.50 at the nearest deli. You can do even better, turning mere water into sparkling wine! For example, if you elected to drink filtered tap water instead of bottled water every day, you could purchase champagne every weekend with your savings. Consider how much you spend on gourmet coffee and lunches eaten on the run during the business day. By packing a lunch and a thermos daily, you could afford a gracious dinner out every weekend. Whatever your tastes, budget to invest in real pleasures. Having fresh flowers around the house lifts my spirits. They are no less beautiful purchased from the supermarket.

I will skip my sermon that the best things in life are free in favor of arguing that enjoyment need not be expensive. So much of luxury is only for display, and the rich are notoriously inefficient about indulging their pleasures. In 1897, during America's Gilded Age, the hosts of a memorable New York party proudly announced that the party cost them millions (in today's dollars). One guest, August Belmont, came to the party in a suit of gold-inlaid armor, which he discarded before the evening was out and never donned again. Needless to say, no one is around to wax nostalgic about the fun that they enjoyed at such frivolous expense.

Elegance is not for sale at any price. When the impoverished Audrey Hepburn moved with her mother from war-torn Belgium to London to study dance, her entire wardrobe consisted of a black blouse, skirt, slacks, and slippers. Nevertheless, her well-heeled classmates voted her the most elegantly dressed student. Her secret was this: wearing a different, brightly colored scarf each day.

Of course, those who make a business of transforming the ordinary into the elegant charge outrageously for the pleasure. Christian Delouvrier, the soft-spoken chef of New York's exclusive restaurant, Lespinasse, defended the $35 price of a bowl of his potato-and-leek soup because it contained truffles. "I pay $1,600 a pound for my Italian truffles," he argued. "You can pay less, of course, but then they would not be as good." He acknowledged that "without the truffles, the soup would probably cost maybe $10 or $12."[6] I must confess that potato-and-leek soup is my favorite kind of soup and that my wife makes it in great freezable batches (alas, without truffles) for mere pennies. Elegant but affordable luxuries can get to be a regular habit once you decide to enjoy yourself more.

BASIC PLEASURES

Singles can suffer the nagging temptation of suspecting that other people are enjoying themselves more than they are and of therefore feeling deprived. My father, the mildest of men, persuaded himself that, were it not for the responsibilities of work and family and the constraints of Christianity, he would have been the wildest playboy of the Western world. Instead, he was dutiful, but he indulged in simple pleasures. In growing season, Dad would pick a flower from our garden and wear it in his buttonhole all day at the office. That small gesture acknowledged the gifts of his Creator and made his day's work more a piece with the rest of his life. Stop to smell the flowers. Occasionally wear a blossom.

Despite their hankering for the freedom to indulge themselves in retirement, most Americans—single as well as married—do not move to warm-weather paradises but remain contentedly in the homes in which they pursued their working lives. They realize that friends, neighbors, churches, and familiar places offer more reliable pleasures than life among strangers on a beach or golf course.

The lives of the rich and famous, although comfortable, are typically prosaic. William Shatner, who, as Captain James Kirk in *Star Trek*, ventured where no man went before, confides that he is content to be home alone:

I don't live an extravagant lifestyle. I don't attend lavish soirées in the south of France, or black-tie events in Manhattan. I stay home. I don't have champagne wishes or caviar dreams . . . I'm thrilled if my fries are supersized. Give me a take-out pizza, a couch full of dogs, and a rented Jackie Chan video and I'm happy as a clam.[7]

Shatner lives in Kentucky rather than Beverly Hills because he raises horses, his one real luxury.

Peter Mayle, whose book, *A Year in Provence*, tempted a generation of Americans to pull up stakes and move to the south of France, is any sybarite's icon. Yet he, too, protests:

I have one house, one small car, one bicycle, and four seldom-worn suits. Food and wine, since I'm lucky to live in an agricultural area of southern France, are good and inexpensive. My vices are relatively cheap, and I spend more money on books than anything else. I have no wish for a yacht, a racehorse, a butler, or even a crocodile attaché case with solid brass fittings and a combination lock, let alone the possessions that really gobble money—a vineyard in Bordeaux, for instance, or a collection of Impressionist art. I can admire and appreciate all these wonderful things, but I don't want to own them. They are, as far as I am concerned, more trouble than they're worth. They end up owning you.[8]

A few years ago, I set about writing a book about the pursuit of happiness. When I was finished, it turned out to be a recipe for simple living, including a large dose of spirituality. Along the way, I discovered, as Mayle did, that nonessential possessions weigh one down and distract the mind and senses, which need to be free to concentrate on contentment. I suggest that you conduct a substantial yard sale to rid yourself of excess possessions that clutter your life. Invest the proceeds in something that gives you pleasure.

PERILS OF PRIVILEGE

Some people suspect pleasure to be sinful. I disagree. The ascetical undercurrent in much of religion must be understood for what it is: not a denial of enjoyment, but only a determination not to be distracted from what truly matters. There is wisdom in the old saying: "The good is the enemy of the best."

Monks live simple lives because they focus totally on the Creator of all good. They pursue perfect joy: "Eye has not seen nor ear heard, nor has it entered the mind of man, what God has prepared for those who love him" (1 Cor. 2:9). Incidentally, some of the most flavorful (albeit uncomplicated) meals that I have eaten have been in seminaries and monasteries. Clearly, some pleasures are harmful, and even otherwise innocent pleasures can be harmful in excess, but that is no reason to fault enjoyment itself.

Of course, some people demand too much of pleasure, especially the kind that they pay much for. Peter Mayle, who has earned his living from profiling the rich and famous, acknowledges:

After pressing my nose up against the window and watching them in action . . . I'm not at all sure that they enjoy themselves as much as we think they do. And why? Because expectations tend to increase in direct proportion to the amount of money being spent.[9]

When people spend a fortune, they expect perfection. Alas, life's delivery systems are seldom so efficient as to deliver guaranteed bliss. Luxury automobiles are as subject to recalls as tiny compacts. Hollywood caterer Steve Michelson said of actress Faye Dunaway: "She insists on three different dishes—a meat, a poultry, and a fish dish—with all the trimmings. She tastes all three, decides which one she wants, and sends the other two back."[10] Comedian Mike Myers, according to Michelson, once threw his chicken dinner all over his trailer because it was too salty. On the other hand, actors Eddie Murphy and Johnnie Depp pass up catered meals on

Hollywood sets for the simpler pleasures of McDonald's, Burger King, and KFC. Clint Eastwood stands in the buffet line with the rest of his cast and crew. They are seldom discontented, whereas spoiled people are seldom satisfied.

Despite the volume and variety of cooking shows on television, only 16 percent of U.S. families who eat at home do their own cooking, opting instead for commercially prepared meals and carryouts. Singles and families with incomes of $70,000 or more spend more money in restaurants than on their groceries.[11] Executives in the nation's capital often install state-of-the-art kitchens in their homes but use only the microwave for the rare at-home meal.

At Mount Vernon, George and Martha Washington dined, of necessity, by candlelight. Americans did not even begin thinking candlelit dinners to be romantic until the era of electric lighting. Now they are. When was the last time that you enjoyed such a simple pleasure at such little expense as candlelight?

WHAT'S WRONG WITH THE WORLD?

Following World War I, the *Times* of London asked prominent writers of the day to submit essays on the topic, "What's wrong with the world?" G. K. Chesterton responded to the question with a single word: "Me!" He was answering, of course, not only for himself, but for much of humanity. Chesterton was persuaded that people spoil life for themselves and for one another by being self-centered and shortsighted.

Still, the portly pundit was no Puritan. Rather, he acknowledged that the most rewarding pleasure comes from pleasing one another. There is nothing new here. It is only the Golden Rule restated as acting for the common good. Formal invitations to gatherings used to request "the pleasure of your company," expecting their guests to be a pleasure. Long before movies, television, and video games turned us into solitary couch potatoes, people entertained one another with their conversation, companionship, and simple presence. Reading a nineteenth-century guest book discovered in a Connecticut home that my family borrowed one summer, I was struck by the sentiments that visitors recorded there so long ago, thanking their hosts and fellow guests for pleasant sojourns together. Clearly, people once took pleasure in one another's company and were openly grateful for companionship.

People still socialize, of course, but much of human intercourse today revolves around business, sports, or other busy agendas. Every Saturday in fair weather, our local school's playing field hosts hundreds of tiny soccer players and their cheering parents. Lamentably, the games are not occasions for couples to enjoy the company of other adults. Their kids' competition is the only point for gathering in the same place at the same time. They scarcely talk with one another. They might as well be living alone, as singles do.

Early in my working life, when I first became a supervisor, I was advised not to socialize much with my coworkers, lest I be accused of currying or granting favors to some and not to others. In retrospect, I must admit that it was wise counsel, because I had to make some painful employment decisions about some of my professional colleagues. But those constraints severely restricted my circle of friends and created barriers to widening my circle of friends. Over time, I found myself wearing one face to work and another in my personal life.

Churches still afford singles and marrieds the opportunity to socialize and support one another. Lending assistance and giving pleasure are much the same thing. But it is as easy to compartmentalize worship and fellowship as anything else in life. Today, my wife and I are fortunate to worship with a small meeting of Friends who minister to one another. There is no posturing or phony piety among us, just pleasing honesty.

Books are still being written for singles that purport to tell them how to be make themselves attractive to each other, but their prescriptions are typically contrived. To be truly pleasing involves more than learning the latest pickup lines. Once upon a time, there were "charm schools" that taught young women to be interesting and pleasing. Our eldest daughter attended one such course and learned a variety of things that make her a person whom others find attractive. She is often accused of being "too friendly," opening herself to being rebuffed by strangers. But she persists.

I am haunted by a study made by Robert Bellah in 1985 (published as *Habits of the Heart*), in which the sociologist profiled an entire American population that, despite material comfort, still lacks a language in which to express longings, moral purposes, and the meaning of life.[12] If you can't please yourself, you can't please others or open yourself to their wanting to please you. Determine to be the kind of person who pleases. It will afford you with the most satisfying pleasures of all.

AN ARRAY OF ENJOYMENT

Although there are as many pleasures as there are people to enjoy them, they have little in common. How can you compare the pleasures of taste with those of sight, smell, hearing, and touch? The calm beauty of a sunset speaks a different message than does the intimacy of lovemaking.

Moreover, what pleases you may bore another, and not just because you face life on your own.

What is crucial is to cultivate a variety of enjoyments. Beyond the primal pleasures of floating in the womb and nursing at the breast, there is the pleasure that comes from the relief of pain and discomfort. I bless my rheumatologist for that joy. Then there are the elemental pleasures of laughter, play, movement, and vocal expression. If you don't sing in the shower, you might consider adding that habit to your repertoire. I know a single mother whose social life is largely restricted to practicing the tango with other dedicated amateurs every Saturday night. No romance is involved, just the love of dancing.

Then there are mental, emotional, sensuous, sexual, and spiritual pleasures that are available to you. All of them can be welcomed into your daily life, but they demand time and attention. Americans of all ages and conditions are addicted to television because its appeal is to "sit back and enjoy." On the other hand, more active pleasures require some personal investment and expenditure of energy and they keep us from becoming couch potatoes.

Enjoyment also requires a sense of humor and adventure and a lighthearted attitude. When people please themselves, they most resemble children at innocent play. Don't ignore your inner child, who wants to get out and have some innocent fun.

Abraham Lincoln was prone to depression, but he was persuaded that "most people are as happy as they make up their minds to be."[13] Psychologist Paul Pearsall suggests that singles test whether they welcome pleasure or resist it. Whether you answer yes or no to the following statements may suggest your personal "pleasure quotient."

People say that I have a nice smile.

Other people smile at me.

I laugh and cry easily.

I take time to reflect on life's gifts.

I avoid conflicts and recriminations.

I avoid replaying past regrets.

I am fun to be around.

I talk about subjects other than work with my co-workers.

I do not hold grudges.

I avoid making critical remarks about people.

I listen to criticism and do not brood over it.

When I go to bed at night, I am grateful for the day.

When I am ill, I stop work and enjoy my recovery.

When alone, I sometimes act silly, dance, and sing.

I do not compare my happiness to that of others.

I don't mind losing, and I congratulate the winners.[14]

Lionel Tiger hails personal optimism as "nostalgia for the future."[15] Of course, we can't be Pollyannas all of the time, but traits such as these keep you open to pleasures both old and new.

PLEASURES THAT INVOLVE OTHERS

There are 500 million vital creatures in American homes in addition to the humans who live there. They are our pets—mostly dogs and cats—and they provide us with the pleasure of their company. Domestic animals demand little from us and seldom complain, while displaying affection and loyalty that are worthy of the saints. Our human behavior is often contrived, whereas beasts act naturally. Studies overwhelmingly demonstrate that owners of pets are happier and healthier and even enjoy lower blood pressure.

Singles living alone not only derive joy from pets, but security as well. Nessie, our Scottish terrier, who barks at the approach of any intruder, dispenses with the requirement to install an electronic security system.

I often ponder how dogs and cats manage to act out their natures so consistently and beautifully when you and I can find it a trial just to act human. Pets are the surest antidote for human loneliness. By being dependent on their masters and mistresses, they also make their owners more responsible. Your best (and cheapest) investment in a more pleasant life may possess a tail. A trip to your local animal shelter will prove my point. You will find it almost impossible to return home alone.

Then there is that other pleasure that requires the presence of another warm living being. Only a human one will do for physical intimacy. Solitary sex is a shallow substitute that can leave you feeling more alone than ever. Self-love is a misnomer in any case. True sensuality is a pleasure that insists on collaboration and reciprocity.

Sex is also demanding: we cannot consume love; we must make it. By choice or circumstance, many men and women who forego expressing themselves sexually find other kinds of emotional intimacy. Some choose to be celibate because they sense that sex distracts them from a more prized pursuit.

Without disputing the power of sex to please, a case can be made that its need is highly overrated. When the pleasure is added up over a lifetime, a man or woman who enjoys sexual intercourse twice a week between the ages of eighteen and seventy-two will have reached the peak of ecstasy for a total of only nine hours and twenty minutes.

Given the choice between foregoing the pleasures of sex and losing the enjoyment of the other senses, sex loses hands down. There can be no contest between a rare, ecstatic pleasure and the more common but continuous and renewable delights of sight, hearing, taste, and touch. Sex is vulnerable to serious abuse when it is separated from love. It is an enjoyment that cannot be served or consumed like junk food.

Here is what Thomas Moore, a psychiatrist and former celibate monk, said about this most intimate pleasure:

In sex, an inner me of strong emotions and vivid fantasies meets with a real person to create a moment of exceptional intensity when life is full and reason is dim. It is a time when play is paramount and yet when nothing could have more serious implications. Even when sex is not ecstatic or perfect, it takes us to a level far from the mundane. Gaze and touch induce a kind of trance, an altered state of consciousness, a realm of imaginal sensations and events, a separate reality. The soul craves such excursions from literal reality, and so it is no mystery that sex is so compelling and enticing. But it is the soul, and not some inanimate body, that feels the hunger and can't resist the appetite. An altered state, like a sexual trance, is not empty . . . In sex we may subliminally discover many truths about our partner, ourselves, our relationship, passion, and love itself.[16]

BEING RICH

I confess to being a happy man. I often brood and frequently complain, but I am more than content overall. You can be, too. Much joy comes simply from keeping busy and paying attention. George Bernard Shaw claimed, "The way to have a happy life is to be so busy doing what you like all the time that there is no time left to think about whether you are happy."[17]

It helps to count your blessings. The sun plays no favorites, rising on the just and unjust alike. Unless you are deaf, you cannot escape hearing the birds' songs. Unless you are blind, you cannot escape seeing beauty. Each evening it is newly pleasant to sleep and each morning it is refreshing to awake. Your mind and senses are like sponges that are prepared to absorb the next item of interest and the occasional bit of wisdom. Your senses actually strain for pleasure. The world is your playground. For such a life of enjoyment, the only appropriate response is gratitude.

Anthropologist Lionel Tiger celebrates the pervasiveness and inevitability of pleasure:

Certain large themes of human existence are difficult to avoid. They ring in the ear. Pleasure resonates as an imperative. There is no choice but to expect it, experience it, enjoy it. We could not have survived the dark nights and bright days of our immense story without it. It was a guide, a lure, a road sign to an oasis. Its enjoyment summarized good and successful choices, and its experience was a confirmation. It was and is central to our deepest accountancy, finally as clear-cut as the mysterious certainty of soaring music. Pleasure as guide, pleasure as proof, pleasure as tonic, pleasure as festivity, pleasure as fun and as triumph. There's no choice. We have to have pleasure.[18]

To be sure, not everyone agrees, concerned that mere pleasure may distract you from deeper satisfaction. Robert Barclay, the seventeenth-century Quaker theologian, condemned not only violence, but "games, sports, plays, comedies, or other recreations which are inconsistent with Christian silence or gravity."[19] He specifically condemned "drunkenness, whoring, and riotousness," and would probably get no argument on those latter counts. But three centuries later, there is a piano in the Quaker meetinghouse where my wife and I worship, and our fellow members occasionally burst into song during our otherwise silent meetings. Children play in the little graveyard behind the simple old building, and there is much laughter among the adults.

In her childhood, my wife was taught this poem:

Quaker meeting has begun.
No more laughing, no more fun.
If you chance to crack a smile,
You will have to walk a mile.

As adults, we have discovered otherwise. The gentle Friends delight in the human comedy, laughing first of all at themselves. They are grateful for simple gifts, not least the gift of enjoyment.

To be sure, happiness consists of more than the accumulation of pleasures. Joy is nourished by virtue. Because he possessed faith, hope, and love, St. Paul, in prison, without spouse or children and deprived of nearly every pleasure, could nevertheless exclaim, "Now I have everything I want—in fact I am rich" (Philippians 4:18).

You may be single, but you are not alone. If you will count your blessings, you will discover that you are rich.

RESOURCES

De gustibus non est disputandum is a fancy way of saying that only you can be the judge of what gives you pleasure. So, unlike previous chapters, there are no Web sites or toll-free numbers here to assist you in your pursuit of happiness. For all I know, you may fancy Cuban cigars, or walks in the wilderness, or gold-plated bathroom fixtures. If so, you already know where to look to indulge your interests. I would only urge you to look around and note what pleases other people, to be open to a wider world of enjoyment, and, of course, to find pleasure in pleasing others. Enjoying the world is your proper compliment to its Maker.

Having said that, I must acknowledge that there are writers who relish the subject of enjoyment. Here are a few books worthy of your perusal:

David G. Myers, *The Pursuit of Happiness* (Morrow, 1992)

Lionel Tiger, *The Pursuit of Pleasure* (Little, Brown, 1992)

Peter Mayle, *Acquired Tastes* (Bantam, 1992)

Thomas Moore, *The Soul of Sex* (HarperCollins, 1998)

Stella Resnik, *The Pleasure Zone* (Conari Press, 1997)

Andrew M. Greeley, *Faithful Attraction* (Tor/St. Martin's, 1991)

And, if I may add, my own *Spiritual Simplicity* (Simon & Schuster, 1997).

11

Write Your Own Script for Living

Happiness depends upon ourselves.

Aristotle

It's crunch time to begin writing the script for the single life in which you are the star. No one else can do it for you, nor would you wish them to. There's only one you to satisfy, after all and no one should know you better than yourself.

When scripting your life, be sure to leave room for lows as well as highs when you're on your own. Here's a cautionary tale:

Just after Grace Kelly, the future princess of Monaco, was presented with the Academy Award for best actress in 1954, she retired alone to her bungalow in the Bel Air Hotel. Her father phoned, but only with backhanded congratulations. He had never much appreciated his daughter and told his friends, "I simply can't believe Grace won. Of the four children, she's the last one I'd expected to support me in my old age."

Grace, all alone, confessed: "This is the one night I wished I smoked and drank."

Robert Lacey, Kelly's biographer, completes the story of that less-than-celebratory occasion:

It was the small hours of the morning . . . She was all alone, with only her Oscar for company, and she set the little metal manikin on the top of her dressing table. She lay down on the bed, she later remembered, and looked across the room at the statuette that represented so much effort and hope and sacrifice, the culmination of her life and work to that point. "There we were," she recalled, "just the two of us. It was terrible. It was the loneliest moment of my life."[1]

LIVE ALONE AND LIKE IT

Before you and I can be free to do as we please, we must determine what it is that makes us happy. Many people don't really know what might truly satisfy them. Instead, they are content to blame their unhappiness on constraints in their lives that are imposed by other people. Tal Ben-Shahar teaches the most popular class at Harvard University, attracting one of every five students on the Cambridge campus. It is a course on how to be happy. He calls one of his bits of practical wisdom the "lasagne principle," which states that "our capacity to enjoy different activities is limited and unique."[2] Professor Ben-Shahar's favorite food is lasagne, prepared by his mother. But, he confesses, he doesn't want lasagne all day every day:

The same principle applies to my favorite activities, such as writing and watching movies, as well as to my favorite people. Just because my family is the most meaningful thing in my life does not mean that spending eight hours a day with them is what would make me happiest; and not wanting to spend all my waking hours with them does not imply that I love them any the less. I derive a great deal of pleasure and meaning from being with other people, but I also need my daily quota of solitude. Identifying the right activity, and then the right quantity for each activity, leads to the highest quality of life.[3]

The only method for determining what makes each of us happy is trial and error. Experimenting ensures that we will make mistakes, but our errors need not be life-threatening. Ben-Shahar quotes Henry David Thoreau, who observed that "Life is too short to be in a hurry."[4]

Ask yourself whether you keep so busy that you are only reacting to persons and events, rather than acting on your own wishes. "Busy-ness" is a chronic form of avoidance, whereby we cling to old habits rather than test them for the pleasure that they afford us. It's a form of escapism, whose underlying principle is "Better the devil you know than the one you don't." Granted, there's nothing wrong with being in a rut, as long as it's a happy one—but most ruts aren't particularly happy. And there don't have to be "devils" in your life.

KEEPING TRACK OF YOUR PLEASURES

Once upon a time, I worked for a prominent public relations firm whose earnings came wholly from billing clients for the time that our staff devoted to their accounts. Time was money. As a consequence, I was required at the end of each day to inform the office's master computer which client to bill for every 15-minute segment of my workday.

That discipline had the effect of sharply abbreviating my lunch and bathroom breaks, but it forced me to account for my time. Admittedly, not every quarter-hour of my labor on behalf of a client was equally productive. Nor can I vouch for the value of my daydreaming.

Even earlier in my career, without any prior experience, I was thrust into service as the academic dean of a liberal arts college. After a couple of weeks of just reacting to the work that came over my desk, I decided to chart how I was spending my time. Predictably, I discovered that I was spending an equal amount of time on things that mattered much less than others. So I began to prioritize my tasks, with the result that I not only began to use my time more effectively but derived more satisfaction from my workday.

To get a handle on the totality of your life and make it more satisfying, start keeping track of how you are actually spending your time. Keep a brief record of your daily activities, and then assign each of them two letter "grades": (1) How meaningful was the activity? (2) How much pleasure did you derive from it? For example, eating is a pleasure at any time, but it can also have meaning if it is a shared lunch or dinner with friends. If it's merely a fast-food meal, devoured in haste, it will be neither meaningful nor especially pleasure-giving. Here's a cautionary note: Don't be too hard on yourself. If you were content to just goof off part of the day, admit it. But ask yourself: How much did I enjoy it?

Give the experiment in daily record-keeping two weeks at a minimum; then sit back and assess how much time you are devoting to activities that are neither meaningful nor very satisfying. Then begin to adjust your priorities to favor yourself. Don't excuse yourself from more enjoyment by pretending that your life is controlled by your family or job and consists simply of obligations. And don't dismiss this exercise as being silly and selfish. Unless you are good to yourself, you can't be good for other people. Philanthropy begins at home. Any script for a satisfying single life not only starts but ends with you.

ELEMENTS OF EVERY SCRIPT

My wife, a writer of mysteries, is bound by many rules of plotting, characterization, and dialogue. Although her novels are products of her imagination, she invests more time and effort on making her fiction true to life than I spend on research for my nonfiction books. Moreover, her readers demand that her books be filled with surprises and suspense, not to mention danger.

In writing your script for living on your own, you must rely on your imagination. But your life is fact, not fiction. Here are some requirements that everyone must take into account:

1. Conduct an honest self-assessment that incorporates your living skills. Living on your own, you require more skills than just knowing how to change a light bulb. Get yourself an inexpensive tool kit and a simple repair manual. Keep your expectations of comfort both high and reasonable. If you want your home or apartment to be clean and orderly, you have to establish a routine to keep it that way. The same is true for laundry and dry cleaning. Good habits are as easy to acquire as bad ones. Establish routines for shopping, banking, bill paying, and auto maintenance so that they become second nature. Locate a reliable doctor and dentist, and don't wait for a health tragedy before you pay them a visit. Just because you don't have someone around to nag you doesn't let you off the hook to care for yourself. Life's necessities need not be burdens. You alone are responsible for making your life pleasant. Learn to cook for yourself and for others. Good meals are among life's most reliable pleasures. Look at yourself in the mirror and smile.

2. Assess your ability to support yourself financially. Unless you're destitute, you can live simply and comfortably without assuming the constant burden of debt. Most working people live paycheck-to-paycheck, but they are sure that the next paycheck is coming. A mortgage is the only substantial debt worth taking on, because it allows you a choice of where to live, the satisfaction of ownership, and equity, which is a form of savings. To go into substantial, long-term debt to buy a new car is something else altogether. The car loses values as soon as you drive it off the lot, and it keeps losing value. Better to drive a clunker purchased for cash than to go into debt. Put something from every paycheck into savings, and plan for emergencies. They are predictable. (You just don't know what, when, or how costly.)

3. Ask yourself whether you are content where you live. Everyone, rich and poor, lives within four walls, but the resemblance ends there. Make sure that your living space reflects and satisfies you. Add color and choose comfortable furnishings. Paint and even wallpaper are easy to apply. A comfortable couch may be a better choice than the largest-screen television that you can find. If you lack imagination, go to the public library and peruse books on home furnishing. Add plants and a pet if they suit you. When you walk into a pleasant home, you know that it reflects the happiness of the people who live there. Most likely, you live where you do because of your job or because, later in life, you prefer to remain in familiar surroundings and with friends that you've made over the years. However . . .

4. Decide for yourself whether the grass is greener elsewhere. Don't wait until retirement to move to the place that you've always dreamed of. You have one life and no one to tie you down. Unfortunately, although singles are free to roam, they can be shy about traveling on their own. But unless you move around and sample

some modest adventures, you are, in effect, your own prisoner and inclined to complain, "Is this all there is?" If you still want to explore prospects for marriage, make sure that you live in a place with such prospects. In any case, take trips with friends. Those adventures will not only be safer but cheaper than those that you take solo. But don't expect a move to be an escape. We seldom escape our circumstances and never escape ourselves. More about that in the next chapter.

5. Who will come to your assistance when needed? Your script for single living calls not only for a good plot but good characters. Even though you're single, you're not a one-man or one-woman band. You must assemble a supporting cast that you can depend on.

No matter whether you're an elderly widow or a young NFL linebacker, there will be occasions when you need personal assistance from others, and it won't be as easy as paying a plumber to fix a leak. You need favors from friends. Bridget Jones's fear that she would be found dead in her flat days after being eaten by dogs is not realistic. But who will you call on if you're sick and need a ride to the doctor or emergency room? Who can you count on for meal preparation and shopping if you are temporarily bedridden? Who will pick up your prescriptions? If your car breaks down, who will give you a lift while it's in the shop? If you decide to move, who can you call on to help you? Don't wait for emergencies to occur and then rely on the kindness of strangers. Many, if not most, of the men and women who reside in nursing homes are not helpless, but friendless. They could still be living comfortably on their own if they had cultivated friends who could help out in a pinch. Incidentally, if you belong to a church, there are volunteers who serve as friends in need. But you have to ask.

SCRIPTS TO SUIT YOUR OWN CIRCUMSTANCES

No two singles, male or female, are alike. Once you possess the skills and security that are necessary for living comfortably on your own, you still are both enabled and constrained by your particular life situation. The man or woman just out of college writes a script for single living that is different from that of a single mother or father, a widow or widower, or a man or woman who was once married but now divorced. Nevertheless, all of them have this in common: they are each on their own and they need a script.

SCRIPTING FOR YOUNG SINGLES

Single life is not necessarily easier for those who are young and unattached. Many young people are burdened with debt. Many are saddled with jobs that cannot yet be considered "careers." An astounding number of men in their twenties and early thirties still live with their parents.

If any of this describes you, here are some considerations when writing your own script for a satisfying single life:

1. Are you content with being single? I don't just mean "reconciled" to your life alone. Even if you still aspire to married life as a possibility, that fact should not make your present life seem at all second-rate. At the same time, you need to determine how much effort to put into searching for a suitable partner. Contented singles tend to expand their social networks with a view to making reliable and interesting friends of both sexes, young and old. If you do that, you are likely to meet persons who want to be more than just friends with you.

2. How well are you using your freedom? Other men and women your age, however content with their lives, are tied down with spouses and children. You may feel that you are tied down to a job, but you are actually free to invest in adventure. You may be saddled with college or other debts, but you are earning an income, however modest. Spend some of it capitalizing on your freedom. Surely, there are things that you have always wanted to do or places where you wanted to go. Now you are perfectly positioned to do them, and you don't need a significant other to accompany you. Above all, don't allow your life to drift. Don't just wait for something (or someone) wonderful to happen to you. Seniors about to graduate from Dartmouth College are given an exit interview, at which each is asked, "What would you do if you had a million dollars?" Whatever the reply, the graduate is asked, "How could you manage to do it without the million dollars?" Not surprisingly, most of the graduates find a way.

3. Is your family an asset or a liability? That's a harsh question. These are the people who should have your interests at heart. On balance, are they supportive or demanding? Could you abide disappointing them by not completely achieving their hopes for you? The true test of adulthood is the ability to take risks, make mistakes, live with them, and then pick yourself up and start all over again.

SCRIPTING FOR YOUNG SINGLES LIVING TOGETHER

All of the previously described information applies in writing your own script, but you have another character in your cast to consider.

1. Is this living arrangement going anywhere, or are you just marking time? Either way, you'd best not allow your life to drift. You are no less single for sharing a bed with someone you care for. In the short term, it can be reassuring to know that you have someone to return to at the end of the day, but, in the slightly longer term, you require some predictability in your life. Otherwise, you are at the mercy of a relationship and living arrangement that can dissolve at any time.

2. Are you tied down or still free? Do you still see your single friends as often as before and seek new friends and challenges? The big difference between marriage and cohabitation is that you don't know how much exclusivity you owe to (and expect from) the person that you live with. Oddly enough, married couples can be far less demanding of each other because they have made a commitment and can take each other's attention for granted. If you think of living with someone as a "trial marriage," how will you judge whether you have succeeded or failed? In brief, how much uncertainty can you handle and still bounce back as good as new?

3. How likely are you to beat the odds? Few cohabiting couples actually marry. Most such arrangements break up within three to five years. Those who do tie the knot tend to divorce within five years at a rate double that of other marriages. Having children together does not make these marriage any less prone to failure.

SCRIPTING FOR DIVORCED MEN AND WOMEN

Tolstoy famously wrote that "All happy families are like one another; each unhappy family is unhappy in its own way."[5] If that is true, each divorced man or woman feels different from every other. Some consider themselves the victims of their failed marriages. Few blame themselves altogether for the breakup. There are few experiences in life more tragic than two people in love who could not maintain their commitment to each other. Forget the former spouses who claim that they remain best friends with their exes. Most divorces are not only painful but bring out the worst in people who once loved deeply.

1. Get used to the idea that you are a single person. Thinking of yourself as "formerly married" or as an "ex-spouse" mires you in the unhappy past. You are back on your own, however reluctant you were to have your marriage fail. Get "failure" out of your head. Write your new script for single living as if for the first time. If you have children by your former marriage, count that as a plus that other singles lack. No one can take from you the fact that you are a mother or a father.

2. Get your personal finances in order. The most immediate consequence of divorce is that there is less money, a lack that may be eroding your quality of life. Depending on how long you were married, you may have lost the knack of living alone and find single life oppressive. So you have to learn to enjoy freedom all over again. On the other hand, singles can live contentedly in smaller spaces and on smaller budgets. So can you.

3. Create an expanding social life. That doesn't mean jump in a stranger's bed to compensate for the intimacy that you once enjoyed and now miss. On the other hand, don't demonize the opposite sex as being unreliable emotionally just

because of your personal experience. Don't make a new romance a big priority, even if you feel that your physical attractiveness is fading. Everyone's is, and, if the right person comes along in the course of your renewed single life, it won't be a "toy boy" or "trophy wife," but someone close to your age who shares with you the disappointments of divorce. If that "right person" doesn't come along, accept the fact that you are older and set in your ways and wouldn't want to compromise the person that you have become just to have a new mate.

Consider this advice from author Barbara Holland, divorced and in her eighties, living alone in the Blue Ridge Mountains of Virginia:

If we aren't half of a loving couple—and at least for the moment we aren't—then the next best thing is to spend as much time as possible in the company of people we love. When this isn't possible, we can fall back on ordinary, unloved people, just for the ordinary human faces and voices, who just might, in time, upgrade themselves. Work is what gives us our bread and butter, but love keeps us human. Any old kind of love.[6]

SCRIPTING FOR SINGLE PARENTS

If you are a divorced single mother or father, the previous paragraphs apply. If you were never married before you took on the responsibility of parenthood, you may simply feel yourself to be besieged and abandoned. But one thing is certain: you're not alone in the world. You have a child or children, which can be an advantage if you let it be. Any loneliness that you feel is not as acute as that of a divorced husband or wife who never had kids.

Many years ago, when I divorced my first wife, I got custody of our three preteenage daughters. Those were tough times. I drove an old car that continuously spouted smoke from the exhaust, requiring me to add more motor oil every morning. One Sunday, cash was so low that I had to choose between gas for the car and ice cream cones for the kids. Of course, the kids won. Still, I remember it as a happy time. I slept better than I had for years because I was so exhausted at the end of each day. Despite caring for the kids, I felt unburdened and free, with little time to feel sorry for myself. When Becky appeared to marry me and adopt us all, life was complete. That was thirty years ago.

1. Get your finances in order and make the children your collaborators. This is no time to indulge your child or children. Reassure them with your love and your honesty about how much money and time you can spend with them. Be clear about your expectations of them.

2. Don't skimp on your social life. Don't allow your social life to consist of just what you do with your children. Unless there's a fairy grandmother living close by who is willing to care for the kids, you have to budget for babysitting.

3. Remember that you are a single adult, not just a single Mom or Dad. Carve out a life of your own with other adult friends. Don't expend all of your energy on your children. In the long run, they will not appreciate your self-sacrifice.

4. Decide whether you want to marry or re-marry. Dating may be a disappointment and an experiment in desperation: your prospects probably also are divorced and they may have children. If dating leads to sex, how can you manage it while maintaining your self-respect? Were you to re-marry, could you really handle your new spouse's children in addition to your own? Could you bear being a stepmother or stepfather? What expectations and demands would you bring to a new marriage? As you resume a full social life, look to making friends of both men and women who share your interests—in more than just romance.

SINGLE SURVIVORS

Assuming you are single again after years of marriage, you have age to contend with in addition to the loss of your spouse. Any suggestions that I can make here fall far short of being truly adequate, but I have written a book on the subject: *Celebrating the Rest of Your Life* (Augsburg, 2005) and I recommend it to you.

1. Establish routines that keep you in charge of your life. After years of married life, you are accustomed to joint planning and mutual routines. Now that you're on your own, you have the freedom to establish new routines and re-visit your personal expectations for daily living. Much of this consists of nothing more than acquiring new habits that expand your life as a newly single person. Make certain that you understand your financial situation and can handle payments yourself. Ensure that someone will shop for you, pay bills, and file your tax returns if you are unable to do so. Inform your physician that you're now on your own and want to maintain a healthy lifestyle. Don't skimp on your diet or simple pleasures. Recall the sacrifices and compromises that you made during the course of your married life. Perhaps you can now indulge some of those interests.

2. Avoid eccentricity. In general, people are tolerant and forgiving of older persons who become set in their ways. However, what you seek is not forbearance, but friendship. Even old friends and acquaintances may be inclined, out of concern for your loss, to leave you alone. Unless you express your needs to them and to your family, you may think that they are only avoiding you when they actually want to help you get on with your life. When the actor George Clooney expressed his bachelor freedom by keeping a pet pig in his home, Hollywood did not dismiss him as an eccentric. But older singles can effectively isolate themselves from others by their odd and cranky habits. A minority of men and women treat aging as an excuse for no longer caring about how other people think of them. They thereby trade a sunny disposition for isolation.

3. Seek serenity and adventure. Any script for single living in later years must include new initiatives. Widows and widowers enjoy freedom from their

former responsibilities to employers and their own growing children, becoming almost wholly responsible for themselves. Don't allow your freedom in later life to restrict your activity and enjoyment. Instead, explore new interests, at the same time making an even better friend of yourself. Don't allow time and isolation to weigh heavily on your life alone. Allow others to benefit from your wisdom and relative security. That means volunteering to assist others.

A GOOD SCRIPT

At the beginning of this book, I borrowed some wisdom from the American poet Walt Whitman:

This is what you shall do:
Love the earth and sun and animals,
despise riches,
give alms to everyone who asks,
stand up for the stupid and crazy,
devote your income and labor to others,
hate tyrants,
argue not concerning God,
have patience and indulgence towards the people,
take off your hat to nothing known or unknown,
or to any man or number of men
go freely with powerful uneducated persons, and with the young,
and with the mothers of families
re-examine all you have been told in school or church
 or in any book,
 and dismiss whatever insults your own soul;
and your very flesh shall be a great poem,
and have the richest fluency,
not only in its words
but in the silent lines of its lips and face,
and between the lashes of your eyes,
and in every motion and joint of your body.[7]

You might wish to consider incorporating Whitman's wisdom into your own script for life.

12

Become Your Own Best Friend

One of the bits of false wisdom that I was taught in college was that everyone acts out of self-interest. When I challenged a professor that selfishness could not possibly explain the Christian martyrs going to their death in the arena, he dismissed my objection. "Their faith was their self-interest," he said.

Sorry, but if self-interest were everyone's motive, we would be able to predict people's behavior, whereas, in real life, people are frustratingly unpredictable—sometimes cowardly, occasionally heroic, often expansive, and otherwise petty. But we are seldom purely self-indulgent.

Perhaps completely self-centered men and women already believe themselves to be their own best friends. They are misguided. Selfish people act childishly when they fail to get instant satisfaction. Rather than attract others to them, they isolate themselves from prospective companions who might enrich their lives.

Moreover, the self-indulgent are typically clueless about weathering life's vicissitudes. Demanding immediate satisfaction, they easily fall prey to addictions that can destroy them. In any case, it is not at all in your self-interest to be self-indulgent.

LEARNING TO LIKE YOURSELF

It is better to accept the fact that you are flawed, neither saint nor sinner, but a mixed bag of strengths and weaknesses—sometimes generous, occasionally stingy, often deft, occasionally clumsy. But you are likeable for all that. Your friends are satisfied with you as you are. If you were perfect, you would be intolerable. It's not surprising that the best humor is self-deprecatory, because it faces the facts of the human condition. When you take yourself lightly, you allow others to love you deeply.

English novelist Sally Brampton defines intimacy as "the admission of human frailties on both sides." Close friends adopt an "equal-vulnerabilities policy," neither dominating the other person nor trying to rescue him or her. A therapist told Brampton that "soul mates" are "two people who recognize the damage in each other."[1] That may be an exaggeration. Nevertheless, the most important person that you need to win over is yourself. To do so does not require you to be wonderful—only honest, fair, and generous, with an appropriate sense of humor and fun. Are you clumsy? So was the great pundit G. K. Chesterton, who didn't allow his awkwardness to deter him from attempting everything that interested him. "Anything worth doing," he concluded, "is worth doing badly."[2]

People who are resettled and have their names changed through the Witness Protection Program do not thereby become different persons. Much as you may wish to take a vacation from your current circumstances, regrets, and even guilt—wherever you go, you are still in your own skin and head. You cannot escape yourself, so you must learn to like yourself.

KNOW THYSELF

Plato inherited this tidy piece of wisdom from his teacher Socrates. Unless we first know ourselves, we will have a skewed appreciation of everything and everyone else, and we may be inclined to create a phony, defensive self that others cannot penetrate. If you are prone to be unhappy, it may not be because of your circumstances, but a reflection of your unrealistic self-image and expectations.

One of the valuable features of married life is that it reveals the spouses to each other, warts and all. Married people cannot hide from each other. They are, figuratively speaking, unmasked and, literally, caught with their pants down. Some marriages falter because the spouses cannot abide sharing life with someone who is not overwhelmed by their wonderfulness. But those who honestly acknowledge their frailties learn to concentrate on their strengths. Few people are really evil, but all of us can develop annoying habits that are easy to drop if someone would only alert us to them.

People who can afford the services of a therapist usually are seeking advice on what to do to be happier. But as Sally Brampton acknowledges, "Nobody can do that. A therapist certainly can't." She advises the following:

All a therapist can do is encourage us to know our true selves. The best therapist is ruthless. They see the truth in us and reflect it back. They make our feelings conscious—but only if we are honest enough to reveal ourselves fully. From there on, the hard work is down to us. We need to know ourselves to make honest choices. Facing up to ourselves is painfully hard work. Good therapy is not comfort and consolation; it is challenge and confrontation.[3]

I have spent much of my working life in what is called the "nonprofit" sector. Almost by definition, people who toil for nonprofits do not do so for the money, but because they want to serve people and make the world a better place. They tend to think of themselves as idealistic and self-sacrificing, doing more than their fair share for only modest remuneration. When they are not saving the whales or the environment, they are rescuing people in need. Here, again, is some cautionary counsel from Sally Brampton, writing in the *Sunday Times* of London:

To strengthen the false self and protect the fragile inner self, we may become compulsive helpers and people-pleasers—anything to take the focus off ourselves and put it on other people. We promote ourselves as Mr. or Ms. Wonderful. People don't dare criticize or question us because of all the good work we do ... If we can make people focus on what we do, not what we are, we distract them from the real picture.[4]

A wise priest once said that the human race can be divided into two categories: the "helpers" and the "helpees." He warned me not to expect the latter to overwhelm their benefactors with gratitude, because they do not relish their dependency. As the Old Testament warns: "The mouth bites the hand that feeds it." Once the needy are strong enough, they may come to resent their erstwhile rescuers as oppressors.

When a man addicted to being a helper of the weak and afflicted complained to Sally Brampton that none of them cared to befriend him, she advised him to start cultivating his own friendship: "You sound like a very nice man," she said. "Take comfort. You don't need to look far. He's right there with you."[5]

THE ADVANTAGES AND DISADVANTAGES OF FAMILY

Don't be too quick to rely on your family as a substitute for friends who support you in your single life. Family can actually be an impediment to your contentment—judging your single life to be deficient and even making extra demands on you. Your friends are more likely to accept you as a co-equal, as well as more likely to be understanding of the needs, practical and emotional, of single living.

If you have never married, it's likely that your parents have fretted about you aging alone. If you have siblings who are married, you may note that your parents treat them more like the adults that they are, while treating their grandchildren as rewards for the trials of raising their own children. In the minds of such parents, your single status is evidence that you are still a child. What's worse, they are inclined to turn to you first for help before they approach your married siblings, rationalizing that you don't share their responsibilities for child care and are just sitting around with plenty of time on your hands.

The same thinking motivates employers to expect single employees to work overtime, while permitting married co-workers to leave work early to tend to their children and enjoy first choice of annual leave dates. That is all the more reason for you to cultivate yourself as your own best friend and to assert your right to be treated as an individual.

DEMYTHOLOGIZING THE SINGLE LIFE

Monks, nuns, and priests are revered for committing themselves to the single life. It is assumed that they chose to be single in order to be better able to serve others, whereas those who lack such spiritual motivation for remaining single are widely assumed to be selfish or unlucky in love. Until society adjusts to the fact that most men and women nowadays are unmarried and living productive, satisfying lives, there will be a lingering prejudice against singles.

If you are male and of marriageable age, you may be suspected by strangers of being gay. If you are an aging, unattached woman, you may be assumed to be unattractive to men. Unmarried women have always been judged more harshly than their male counterparts, the common assumption being that "confirmed bachelors" could be married if they wished to be. As it is, there are only 86 unmarried men for every 100 unmarried women in the United States, regardless of their sexual preferences.[6]

Social psychologist Bella DePaulo affirms that the single life is still stigmatized. She has devoted herself to debunking "all of the subtle and not-so-subtle ways in which single people are dismissed, marginalized, and denigrated."

Happily, help is on its way. Singles now have a public policy organization pledged to leveling the playing field. Thomas Coleman is executive director of Unmarried America, which advocates equal rights for singles.

He notes that singles suffer not only unfair work policies, but tax codes that penalize them, higher auto insurance rates, and federal laws that outlaw most forms of discrimination except for those based on marital status.

For example, corporate pensions and Social Security payments automatically benefit a surviving spouse. But if a single person dies before reaching retirement age, benefits cannot be assigned to another person. They are simply lost. Family medical leave typically allows an employee to care for a spouse or child, but not an ailing sibling. Those inequities need to be remedied.

At the moment, singles are twice as likely to lack health coverage as married Americans, whereas spouses who are not employed are typically covered by the employee benefits enjoyed by their working husband or wife.

Over time, employers will be forced to offer long-term-care plans for single employees who lack children to support them in old age. Incidentally, it is largely a myth that children help support their parents in old age—only 15 percent of parents can rely on financial support from their kids.[7]

"SO, WHEN ARE YOU GOING TO GET MARRIED?"

Even strangers casually assault singles with this unkind question, although they would never summon the effrontery to ask a married couple, "So, when are you going to get divorced?" The question assumes that everyone wants to be married, because marriage brings happiness. An unspoken subtext is that to be married also proves that you are grown up and responsible.

Unfortunately, it is not quite that simple. In polls of married and unmarried women, the singles report that they are happier. Although Americans express misgivings about divorce, they have a higher regard for a divorced woman than for her single sister. As Bella DePaulo remarks of public opinion, "If you've been married and divorced, you've shown that you're capable of being loved."[8] On the other hand, people wonder about the still-single person: "What's your flaw that you never got married?" The "flaw" may very well consist of being not at all interested in finding a mate.

In 2007, the Pew Internet and American Life Project reported that a majority (55 percent) of single men and women across the nation have no active interest in seeking a partner. The same poll revealed that only 16 percent of singles are actively looking for love. That does not mean that they are withering on the vine emotionally. More than one in four singles is currently in a committed relationship short of marriage. And others enjoy a rich emotional life through friends and interests.[9]

Duke University sociologist Philip Morgan believes that it is no longer true that single people must want to be married. He suggests that Americans should now consider the possibility that the single life, once only a way station, is becoming a permanent destination.[10]

Advertisers are paying attention. Until recently, they ignored singles once they were out of their teens and on their own. Now companies are beginning to see a vast market out there. DeBeers, which relies on the demand of women for diamond engagement rings, now urges single women to buy their own right-hand diamond rings. Conde Nast created *Men's Vogue* because it realized that single men don't consult women to tell them what to wear and how to dress. More than one in five homes nationwide is now purchased by a single woman for herself.

Increasingly, singles of both sexes view marriage not as a panacea, but as a project. The National Marriage Project reports that 86 percent of young adults believe wedded life is hard work and a full-time job. More than four of five young adults agree that it is unwise for women to look to marriage for their financial security.[11]

LEAVING THE DOOR OPEN FOR LOVE

Singles are increasingly aware that marriage is not a solution to the challenges of living on their own. Rather, marriage can itself be a problem if they merely settle for living with someone whom they don't fully love, respect, and even admire, and who reciprocates in kind. Becoming your own best friend requires you to put your own interests first, not settling for second best. There are sufficient compromises in married life without compromising with yourself by wedding someone who is not worthy of you. You do not have to be overwhelmed by your own wonderfulness in order to discover that someone who loves you. But you can't make it happen either. What you can do is to become your own best friend.

That is something Sally Brampton learned, and love followed in its wake. Brampton, who calls herself "Aunt Sally," makes a living giving advice to the lovelorn, but she was unprepared when love entered her own life unbidden. She was married, for the third time, on Friday the 13th of April 2007, capitulating neither to superstition nor to her previous failures.

"For years," she acknowledges, "I believed I was so hopeless at intimacy that it was best if I stayed single. Then, along came my future husband, and I loved him so much that I slowly learnt the courage and patience it takes to love another person properly."

"Slowly" is her expression for waiting seven whole years of intermittent courtship before taking the plunge. As might be expected, her news was received with something short of enthusiasm. Her teenage daughter said, "Cool," followed by a long pause and then the question "Who to?"

Sally confesses: "When I told my various friends that I was getting married again, only one had the nerve to ask, 'Why?'—the implication being that I am obviously very bad at marriage, so why not just give it up? My closest friend said: 'I think it shows great optimism and an extraordinary willingness to commit.' I love her for that."

She blames the tragedy of her failed marriages on the fact that "I had no idea that love is the ability to share yourself with somebody and to let them share themselves with you, without either of you trying or wanting to change the other."[12]

LIKING YOURSELF

Over the years, I was given responsibility for stage-managing commencement ceremonies at three different colleges. Now and then, my own undergraduate college asked me to be its representative to process with the faculties of other campuses and sit with their graduates. On those occasions, I listened to a lot of commencement addresses from politicians, pundits, celebrities, and captains of industry, each of whom hailed the graduates as our nation's hope, encouraging them to be both ambitious and idealistic in their careers.

But when Barbara Bush addressed my twin daughters' graduating class, the former First Lady sounded an entirely different note. She urged the graduates to look first to their personal lives, not to their careers. She predicted that the value of our lives will be determined not by our résumés, but by the persons who love us and by those whom we have loved and served. Ultimately, she counseled, we must earn our own self-respect.

A similar note was struck by ABC news anchor Charles Gibson, when he addressed graduates of Union College in 2007: "Compassion. Honesty. Fairness. Trustworthiness. Respect for others. If those things are not the bedrocks of your life, you will suffer for their absence in time. And I would wager you won't much like yourself."[13]

Embrace your single life. Take the trouble to earn your own self-respect. You will become your own best friend, and you can join Walt Whitman in approaching life as an adventure:

Afoot and lighthearted, I take to the open road,

Healthy, free, the world before me,

The long brown path before me, leading wherever I choose.[14]

Afterword: It's Never Too Late to Reinvent Your Life

The novelist F. Scott Fitzgerald famously lamented that "there are no second acts in American lives," having persuaded himself that any misstep along the way consigns people to be losers for life. In the spring of 1920, with a successful first novel under his belt and having married the woman of his dreams, the great American novelist confessed that "Riding in a taxi one afternoon between very tall buildings under a mauve and rosy sky, I began to bawl because I had everything I wanted and knew I would never be so happy again."[1] Despite his genius, Fitzgerald managed to fulfil his own prophesy. As his beautiful wife descended into madness, he became a bitter and violent alcoholic, dying prematurely of a heart attack at the age of forty-four.

Fitzgerald's failure might be dismissed as the product of a morbid artistic temperament. But, in our own time, many professional economists echo his pessimism, teaching that all of us are condemned to inhabit a "zero sum" universe, in which life's winners succeed only at the expense of the losers.

Don't believe it. The weight of evidence from the beginning of recorded history demonstrates that the disciples of gloom are dead wrong. Failure is not permanent, but predictable and passing. Every one of us enjoys second chances for success and satisfaction in life, if we will only summon the spirit to grasp them. We may not get everything right the first time, but "starting over" is the American way of life.

Untold millions of men and women have been spurred to success by their setbacks, overcoming the loss of wealth, love, careers, and reputation, successfully compensating for poor health, inadequate education, and even incarceration. Legendary men and women have fought back from financial failure, including Abraham Lincoln, Ulysses S. Grant, and Henry Ford. Winston Churchill was a political has-been during the 1930s, emerging from the shadows to lead his nation to victory in its darkest hour of World War II. Nelson Mandela emerged from years in prison to free his people and become leader of his nation. Against every prediction, Martha Stewart put a prison term behind her to return to the business world as a winner.

Consider this: if the gloom mongers were correct, Jesus of Nazareth would probably rank as history's greatest failure, broken in body and persecuted in spirit, ending his life as a criminal nailed to a cross. But two millennia later, more than 2 billion people across 260 nations call themselves his followers, persuaded that Calvary was only the final scene of Jesus's first act. In the second act of his life, he prevailed over death and won eternity for everyone.

On a less lofty level, countless men and women throughout history have displayed a marvelous resilience in confronting their setbacks and handicaps, turning defeat into victory. Whatever else you may lack, hope should never be among them.

Single Americans can enjoy second chances in love, business, health, education, friendship, and every important aspect of living. The current fashion for "total makeovers" only underscores our confidence that we are the masters of our fate. It will never be too late to start over.

If you sense yourself handicapped in prevailing over failure, it may be because you unconsciously worship at the altar of what psychologist William James called "the bitch goddess of success," narrowly defining personal fulfillment in terms of financial wealth and physical beauty.

Doubtless, we have an impoverished underclass in America, but, as a philanthropic society, we are better than most at providing men and women with the help to hoist themselves by their own bootstraps. Within memory, our nation's large cities consigned the indigent to poor houses. Today, we have the most generous personal and corporate bankruptcy rules in the world, ensuring that penury need not be permanent. Educational opportunity has never been so amply available. We enjoy longer, healthier lives.

America as a society acknowledges personal failure but denies the notion that anyone is a born loser. Christianity, for example, admits distinctions in gifts and accomplishments among God's creatures but affirms that we are all equal in the sight of God. So, if you manage to regard yourself as your designer does, and see what he sees (as in a mirror), you can summon the strength to start over, not just once but many times during your lifetime, reinventing your life.

Your challenge is to identify your alternatives. At any moment, life presents us with a bewildering array of possibilities. Meander down a supermarket aisle, for example, and marvel at all of the shades of hair coloring available. Women who believe blondes have more fun and want more gaiety in their lives can purchase a piece of their future in a box. You're always welcome to reinvent yourself.

Unfortunately, in more serious matters, you may not know what your real alternatives are. People remain in unfulfilling jobs and relationships—not because they are indecisive or lack the courage to extricate themselves from routine, but because they can't conceive of their choices, reverting to being creatures of habit, preferring the devils that they know to the angels that they haven't met as yet. Many of us retreat from our God-given pursuit of happiness too soon, settling for less than we deserve.

Being single, you are unencumbered and freer to explore your options without affecting anyone else. If you hesitate, it may be because you seek more support from others and cannot find it. Alas, others cannot give you the courage to set out on a new path. Friends, family, and colleagues may prefer to keep you around just as you are, leading you to conclude that your present life is your fate.

It's a great irony that sinners and criminals are offered opportunities to start over and take them, whereas better people shy from claiming their own second chances, shrinking from choices that initially may prove to be more unsettling than the ruts in which they already find themselves. Sometimes it takes a serious illness, unemployment, or a personal tragedy to force us to consider our free choices. In such cases, serious setbacks may actually prove to be blessings in disguise.

In our nation's past, people didn't wait for adversity to befall them before taking the initiative to improve their lot. Whole families became pioneers, setting out to seek better lives beyond the next mountain pass, without any assurance of what awaited them. They were motivated by the faith that they could make their new life better than the one that they already knew. Unfortunately, many single Americans are comfortable enough earning a modest paycheck, having a roof over their heads and three square meals a day, without exercising the freedom to change themselves and improve their situations. Ironically, we affluent Americans are settling for less than our impoverished pioneer forebears did.

Caution, habit, and inertia (more often than cowardice) can deter you from choosing a happier life. You would probably reach for the brass ring right now if you knew that it was within your grasp, but what many of us lack is imagination and information. We don't know what our options are, and we fear taking chances. Instead, rather than create our own opportunities, we settle for crossing our fingers, praying that fate will favor us and that opportunity will knock at our door—a prospect less likely than winning the lottery. As Jesus himself noted in the Gospels, for doors to be opened to us, we must first do the knocking.

But at which doors? Maybe it's not at the door that's marked "Marriage." Although Frank Sinatra crooned that love is better the second time around, he married four times, suggesting that wedlock is not the surefire remedy for anyone who feels that his or her single life is emotionally empty.

The nation's divorce courts give evidence that, in matters of love, many otherwise sensible men and women can and do make faulty first choices. To be sure, marriages fail less often for lack of good intentions than for lack of knowledge of one's spouse and the commitment that marriage commands. Sadly, second and subsequent marriages after divorce fail even more frequently than first ones, suggesting that spouses can learn little from their initial experience.

In any case, real success in life doesn't just fall in our laps; it needs to be earned.

If there were a Freedom of Information Act that covered the nation's lotteries, it would reveal that the vast majority of big money winners fail to find happiness. Overwhelmingly, those who win the jackpot run through their prize money, winding up in much the same condition as when they started. Winning the lottery is simply not the great chance to start over that it's cracked up to be. The reason is revealing. Big winners typically quit work altogether and start spending on luxuries—cars, homes, and vacations. In the process, they leave family, friends, and familiar surroundings behind and don't know how to fill their leisure time.

It doesn't take much imagination to realize that such winners are actually poorer for the second chance that the lottery afforded them, because they managed to separate themselves from practically everyone and everything that provided whatever contentment that they knew before they struck it rich.

Starting over calls for engagement, not escape—not for a life of doing nothing, but for a fuller life of doing something satisfying: a better job, a richer education, sounder health, more positive attitude, and a workable faith. You can't purchase those second chances with lottery earnings alone. They take imagination, effort, and information.

Before they graduate, Dartmouth College seniors are each asked to write an essay answering the question, "What would you do if you had a million dollars?" Afterward, each is asked, "How could you accomplish those same goals without the million dollars?" Revealingly, most of the graduates are moved to devise a workable plan, illustrating the fact that we don't necessarily have to invest money in starting over—we only have to invest ourselves!

Second chances are there to be taken, not only in love and work, but in faith, health, education, appearance, attitude, and your choice of domestic life and personal pleasures. But, when you start over, you need to know more than you did when you made your first choices and fell into the routines that define your present life.

My purpose in the previous pages has been to suggest some of the alternatives that are still available to you and how you can grasp them. It's up to you to decide whether you need, or even want, to reinvent yourself and lead a more fulfilled life. You may decide instead to embrace your current life, cultivating a greater appreciation for the blessings that you already enjoy. Other people cannot choose for you; you must decide.

Alarmingly, many single Americans haven't as yet taken their first chances in life but have only drifted into the lives that they lead. Mired in jobs for which they are overeducated and fearful of making permanent emotional commitments, many young singles move back into their parents' home, where they continue to live as aging children. In earlier generations, economic necessity forced young adults to stake out their lives early. Now many can coast in neutral for years, putting their lives on hold, settling for a default existence, without feeling a serious pinch. They do not know what to do with their lives because they do not see the possibilities.

Sometimes we don't see the alternatives because of the emotional state in which we find ourselves. We feel stuck. Or we feel swept along in life, unable to take control.

In my early thirties, I had already failed in the ministry and was struggling to keep a dysfunctional marriage afloat. My three daughters appeared in the first three years of that marriage, all of them born with permanent disabilities, requiring expensive medical care and special education. We were mired in chronic debt. Every morning, when I looked in the mirror, I saw a loser in life. Then a counselor proposed what was a radical fashion for the time: that I grow a beard! His idea was that, from now on, when I looked in a mirror, I would see a different person and be forced to change my outlook. It would also force other people to look at me differently instead of just taking me for granted.

I have the beard to this day. Then it was red; now it's practically colorless. Sure enough, in the early years, I encountered plenty of prejudice because of the fuzz on my face. But my change in appearance shocked me out of my self-pity. Because I looked different to myself and others, I began to develop a different outlook.

Diet counselors insist that, inside every fat person, there's a thin person struggling to get out. Inside you, there is probably someone ready to emerge and start afresh if you only knew what your chances of success might be.

Barbara Walters once told me that her favorite interviews are not with the rich and glamorous, but with statesmen and women with a cause. Leaders know themselves, she said, and they are moved by passion and conviction. Barbara confided that she has found actors and actresses to be the hardest of all for her to interview, because, beneath the roles that they assume on stage and screen, they are often insecure about themselves. Taking second chances in your life rests on having confidence in yourself.

An early feminist tract complained that Audrey Hepburn's screen persona was totally fabricated by Hollywood, just as Henry Higgins shaped the character of Eliza Doolittle, the character the Hepburn played in *My Fair Lady*. I was privileged to meet the actress in her final years before her death from cancer. To be sure, the real-life Audrey Hepburn was shy and inarticulate, not at all like her screen presence. But, by that time, she had already served for years as UNICEF's ambassador to the world's sick and impoverished children. She had chosen a cause, not just accepted a role. She had become her own creature.

From your childhood reading, perhaps you recall that Winnie the Pooh provided a tiny cake for friend Piglet's birthday. "Now blow out all the candles to get your wish," Pooh directed his friend.

"But there's only *one* candle," complained Piglet.

"The better to make your wish come true!" Pooh replied.[2]

Finally, here's some practical wisdom from Sally Jenkins. She is a sports columnist for *The Washington Post*, but what she says about failure and success is true in all of life:

A mistake, while regrettable, is not anything you ever have to repeat again. Every act is redeemable, and the self is not permanent but marvelously supple, and the days ahead are a blank gift in which a person can remake himself in a moment through a single realization, in any fashion he pleases. A fresh start is not something you can demand of others or find via geography, but have to find within.[3]

You, too, can make a fresh start and make your wishes come true—all the more surely by concentrating on them one at a time. The great advantage of the single life is that you are totally in charge of it. I urge you not to be the kind of person who waits for things to happen. Become a person who makes things happen.

Notes

CHAPTER 1

1. Stephanie Irwin, "One: It's No Longer the Loneliest Number," *Dayton Daily News*, September 26, 2006, 15.

2. *Genesis* 2:18.

3. John W. Wright, ed., *The New York Times 2008 Almanac* (New York: Penguin, 2007), 291.

4. Anthony Fiola, "In the New Dating Scene, the Attraction Is a Beautiful Mind," *The Washington Post*, October 15, 2007, A1.

5. Wright, *op. cit.*, 285.

6. David Popenoe, and Barbara Whitehead, "Cohabitation," *National Marriage Project* (New Brunswick, NJ: Rutgers University Press, 2006), 1–2.

7. Wright, *op. cit.*, 287.

8. John Wesley, "Thoughts on Marriage and Celibacy," in *The Life and Times of the Rev. John Wesley, M.A.*, ed., Mike Tyermans (New York: Harper and Bros., 1876), 73 ff.

9. Emily Morison Beck, ed., *Bartlett's Familiar Quotations* (Boston: Little, Brown, 1980), 524.

10. "What Americans Think about Aging and Health," *Parade*, February 5, 2006, 19.

11. Beck, *op. cit.*, 680.

CHAPTER 2

1. "News Notes," *AARP*, January–February 2007, 12.

2. Beck, *op. cit.*, 129.

3. David Yount, "The High Cost of Hooking Up," *Amazing Grace* (Washington: Scripps Howard News Service), June 2, 2004.

4. *Ibid.*

5. Wright, *op. cit.*, 291.

6. Popenoe and Whitehead, *op. cit.*, 1–2.

7. David Reisman, *The Lonely Crowd* (New Haven, CT: Yale University Press), xi.

8. Beck, *op. cit.*, 559.

9. E. Kay Trimberger, *The New Single Woman* (Boston: Beacon Press, 2006), 197.

10. India Knight, "Single and Dangerous," *Sunday Times of London*, December 2, 2007, A17.

11. *Ibid.*

12. Anthony Storrs, *Solitude* (New York: Ballantine, 1988), 63.

13. Louise Bernikow, *Alone in America* (Boston: Faber & Faber, 1986), 11.

14. Helen Fielding, *Bridget Jones's Diary* (London: Picador, 2000), 34.

15. Gina Kolata, "Live Long? Die Young? The Answer Isn't Just in Your Genes," *The New York Times*, August 31, 2006, 37 ff.

16. Beck, *op. cit.*, 887.

17. Martin Seligman, *Authentic Happiness* (New York: Free Press, 2004), 73.

18. D. T. Max, "Happiness 101," *The New York Times*, January 7, 2007, 37.

19. *Matthew* 5:3–12.

20. William Swann, *Self-Traps: The Elusive Quest for Higher Self-Esteem* (Denver: Westview Press, 1996), 69.

21. Elizabeth Wurfel, *Prozac Nation* (New York: Riverhead, 1995), 38.

22. Mark Twain, *The Autobiography of Mark Twain* (New York: Harper Perennial, 2000), 72.

23. Robert D. Richardson, *William James: In the Maelstrom of American Modernism* (Boston: Houghton Mifflin, 2006), 394.

24. Gloria Steinem, *Revolution from Within: A Book of Self-Esteem* (Boston: Little, Brown, 1993), 325.

25. *Ibid.*

26. Jane Fonda, *My Life So Far* (New York: Random House, 2006), 58.

CHAPTER 3

1. Bernikow, *op. cit.*, 11.

2. *Ibid.*, 15–16.

3. *Ibid.*, 72.

4. Irwin, *op. cit.*, 15.

5. Stephen M. Johnson, *First Person Singular: Living the Good Life Alone* (Philadelphia: Lippincott, 1977), 77.

6. *Ibid.*

7. *Ibid.*, 81.

8. Beck, *op. cit.*, 356.

9. Michael Dirda, "Readings," *The Washington Post Book World*, April 22, 2001, 15.

10. *Ibid.*

11. Barbara Holland, *One's Company: Reflections on Living Alone* (New York: Ballantine, 1992), 4.

12. *Ibid.*, 14–15.

13. Johnson, *op. cit.*, 81.

14. *Ibid.*, 133–140.

15. Jennifer Alsever, "In the Computer Dating Game, Room for a Coach," *The New York Times*, March 11, 2007, 38.

CHAPTER 4

1. Christina Breda Antoniades, "Date Lab," *The Washington Post Magazine*, April 22, 2007, 14.

2. Carolyn Hax, "Carolyn Hax," *The Washington Post*, June 7, 2007, C6.

3. Arthur Levine, "Report on Student Relationships," Columbia University Teachers College, Winter, 2006.

4. Laura Sessions Stepp, "Score Card," *The Washington Post*, May 22, 2004, C1.

5. Barbara de Angelis, *The Real Rules: How to Find the Right Man for the Real You* (New York: Dell, 1997), 111.

6. Alice Miller, *For Your Own Good: Hidden Cruelties in Child Bearing and the Roots of Violence* (New York: Farrar, Straus & Giroux, 1190), 21.

7. Frank Pittman, *Private Lies* (New York: W.W. Norton, 1989), 34.

8. Amy Sutherland, "What Shame Taught Me about a Happy Marriage," *The New York Times*, June 25, 2006, 23.

9. Lee Reilly, *Women Living Single: 30 Women Share Their Stories of Navigating Through a Married World* (London: Faber & Faber, 1996), 203.

10. Beck, *op. cit.*, 608.

11. *Ibid.*, 554.

12. Reilly, *op. cit.*, 93.

CHAPTER 5

1. Quoted in Nancy Caro Hollander, ed., *Psychoanalysis, Class and Politics* (New York: Routledge, 2006), 123.

2. Joan Rivers, *Bouncing Back: I've Survived Everything . . . And I Mean Everything . . . And You Can Too* (New York: Harpertorch, 1998), 45.

3. Beck, *op. cit.*, 348.

4. *Ibid.*, 389.

5. *Ibid.*, 88.

6. Harriett Lerner, *Life Preservers: Good Advice When You Need It Most* (New York: Harper Paperbacks, 1997), 289.

7. Tim Plant, "Brave Phyllis Diller Battles Broken Neck with Wisecracks," *Globe*, May 9, 2005.

8. Scott A. Sandage, *Born Losers* (Cambridge, MA: Harvard University Press, 2005), 276.

9. S'Vera Cohn, "Baby Boomers, the Gloomiest Generation," Pew Research Center Publications, June 25, 2008, 1.

10. Wright, *op. cit.*, 285 ff.

11. Joyce Brothers, *Getting the Most from Family Relationships* (New York: Guidance Publishing, 1969), 58.

12. G. K. Chesterton, *Saint Francis of Assisi* (San Francisco: Ignatius Press, 1986), 103.

CHAPTER 6

1. Walter Isaacson, *Einstein: His Life and Universe* (New York: Simon & Schuster, 2008), 178.

2. "Alchemy," *Encyclopedia Britannica* (Chicago: 15th edition), vol. 1, 226.

3. *John* 15:13.

4. Jim Ottaviani, *Suspended in Language: Niels Bohr's Life, Discoveries, and the Century He Shaped* (Ann Arbor, MI: G. T. Labs, 2004), 298.

5. Isaacson, *op. cit.*, 313.

6. Beck, *op. cit.*, 220.

7. *Ibid.*, 560.

8. Bertrand Russell, *Two Modern Essays on Religion* (London: Westholm, 1959), 23.

9. Eric Hoffer, *The Passionate State of Mind and Other Aphorisms* (New York: Hopewell, 2006).

CHAPTER 7

1. "Paul Okalik," *Wikipedia, the Free Encyclopedia,* http://en.wikipedia.org., accessed July 11, 2008.

2. Wright, *op. cit.*, 341.

3. *Ibid.*

4. Beck, *op. cit.*, 743.

5. *Ibid.*, 853.

6. *Ibid.*, 834.

7. Wright, *op. cit.*, 341.

8. *Ibid.*

9. Beck, *op. cit.*, 904.

10. "A Fair Exchange," *Time*, April 28, 1975, 51.

11. "Leiter, on His Way Out, Still Gets Them," *The New York Times*, October 10, 2005, D1.

CHAPTER 8

1. Beck, *op. cit.*, 675.

2. Amanda Scurry, "Good Health Habits Can Be Catching," *University of North Dakota News*, June, 2006, 1–2.

3. Bruno Bettelheim, *The Uses of Enchantment* (New York: Penguin, 1991), 23.

4. Beck, *op. cit.*, 674.

5. Mark Leary, *Interpersonal Rejection* (New York: Oxford University Press, 2001), 241.

6. Joan Collins, *The Art of Living Well* (New York: Sourcebooks, 2006), 124.

7. Robert Byrne, ed., *The 2,548 Best Things Anybody Ever Said* (New York: Fireside, 2003), 426.

8. Beck, *op. cit.*, 315.

9. *Ibid.*, 300.

10. Wright, *op. cit.*, 285.

11. Bernie Siegel, *Love, Medicine, and Miracles* (New York: Harper & Row, 1986), 108.

12. Quoted in David Yount, *Celebrating the Rest of Your Life* (Minneapolis: Augsburg Books, 2005), 102.

13. Wright, *op. cit.*, 285.

14. John Knowles, *Peace Breaks Out* (New York: Holt, Rinehart & Winston, 1981), 5.

15. Yount, *Celebrating the Rest of Your Life*, 107.

CHAPTER 9

1. Wright, *op. cit.*, 324.

2. *Ibid.*, 341.

3. Edna R. Sawady, and Jennifer Tescher, "Financial Decision Making Process for Low-Income Individuals," Joint Center for Housing Studies, Harvard University, February, 2008, 2.

4. *Ibid.*, 3.

5. Andrew Tobias, *The Only Investment Guide You'll Ever Need* (New York: Harvest Books, 2005), 13.

6. *Ibid.*

7. Wright, *op. cit.*, 334.

8. Tobias, *op. cit.*, 23.

9. Jane Bryant Quinn, *Smart and Simple Financial Strategies for Busy People* (New York: Simon & Schuster, 2006), 37.

10. Tobias, *op. cit.*, 212.

CHAPTER 10

1. Quoted in "Style," *Sunday Times of London*, December 1, 1999, 3.

2. Lionel Tiger, *The Pursuit of Pleasure* (Boston: Little, Brown, 1992), 18.

3. David G. Myers, *The Pursuit of Happiness* (New York: Harper Paperback, 1993), 25.

4. Tiger, *op. cit.*, 12.

5. Beck, *op. cit.*, 876.

6. Tiger, *op. cit.*, 143.

7. William Shatner, *Get a Life* (New York: Atria, 1999), 35.

8. Peter Mayle, *Acquired Tastes* (New York: Bantam, 1993), 201.

9. *Ibid.*, 203.

10. *Ibid.*

11. Quinn, *op. cit.*, 38.

12. Robert Bellah, *Habits of the Heart* (Berkeley: University of California Press, 1985), 39.

13. Beck, *op. cit.*, 523.

14. Paul Pearsall, *Write Your Own Pleasure Prescription* (Alameda, CA: Hunter House, 1997), 158.

15. Tiger, *op. cit.*, 288.

16. Thomas Moore, *The Soul of Sex* (New York: Harper Perennial, 1999), 193.

17. Beck, *op. cit.*, 681.

18. Tiger, *op. cit.*, 299.

19. Quoted in John Punchon, *Portrait in Grey* (London: Quaker Home Service, 1984), 131.

CHAPTER 11

1. Robert Lacey, *Grace* (New York: Berkley, 1996), 118.

2. Tal Ben-Shahar, *Happier: Learn the Secrets to Daily Joy and Lasting Fulfillment* (New York: McGraw-Hill, 2007), 41.

3. *Ibid.*

4. Beck, *op. cit.*, 558.

5. *Ibid.*, 602.

6. Holland, *op. cit.*, 241.

7. Walt Whitman, *Leaves of Grass: The Original 1855 Edition* (Mineola, NY: Dover Publications, 2007), i.

CHAPTER 12

1. Sally Brampton, *Shoot the Damn Dog: A Memoir of Depression* (New York: W. W. Norton, 2008), 89.

2. Beck, *op. cit.*, 743.

3. Brampton, *op. cit.*, 127.

4. *Ibid.*

5. *Ibid.*

6. Wright, *op. cit.*, 288 ff.

7. Quinn, *op. cit.*, 47.

8. Bella DePaulo, *Singled Out: How Singles Are Stereotyped, Stigmatized, and Ignored, and Still Live Happily Ever After* (New York: St. Martin's Griffin, 2007), 299.

9. Popenoe and Whitehead, *op. cit.*, 2.

10. S. Philip Morgan, quoted in Dudley L. Poston, Jr. and Michael Micklin, eds. *Handbook of Population* (Boston: Klewer Academic Publishers, 2008), 48.

11. Popenoe and Whitehead, *op. cit.*, 3.

12. Brampton, *op. cit.*, 129.

13. Quoted in "Reliable Source," *The Washington Post*, June 3, 2007, C3.

14. Beck, *op. cit.*, 573.

AFTERWORD

1. Beck, *op. cit.*, 835.

2. *Ibid.*, 778.

3. Sally Jenkins, *The Washington Post*, August 13, 2007, E1.

References

Arnold, William V., and Margaret Anne Fohl. 1990. *When You Are Alone.* Louisville: Westminster/John Knox Press.

Berkinow, Louise. 1986. *Alone in America: The Search for Companionship.* Boston: Faber & Faber.

Farmer, Andrew. 1998. *The Rich Single Life.* Gaithersburg, MD: PDI Communications.

Feldon, Barbara. 2003. *Living Alone and Loving It: A Guide to Relishing the Solo Life.* New York: Fireside.

Holland, Barbara. 1992. *One's Company: Reflections on Living Alone.* New York: Ballantine.

Johnson, Stephen M. 1977. *First Person Singular: Living the Good Life Alone.* Philadelphia and New York: Lippincott.

Kelley, Susan, and Dale Burg. 2000. *The Second Time Around: Everything You Need to Know to Make Your Remarriage Happy.* New York: William Morrow.

Knight, India. 2006. "Single and Dangerous," *The Sunday Times,* December 24, I-18.

Koller, Alice. 1990. *The Stations of Solitude.* New York: William Morrow.

Peterson, Marion, and Diane Warner. 2003. *Single Parenting for Dummies.* New York: Wiley.

Reilly, Lee. 1996. *Women Living Single.* Boston: Faber and Faber.

Reisman, David et al. 1961. *The Lonely Crowd.* New Haven: Yale University Press.

Rubinstein, Robert L., Janet C. Kilbride, and Sharon Nagy. 1992. *Elders Living Alone: Frailty and the Perception of Choice.* New York: Aldine de Gruyter.

Shahan, Lynn. 1981. *Living Alone and Liking It.* New York: Stratford Press.

Sheehy, Gail 1999. *Understanding Men's Passages.* New York: Ballantine.

_____. 2006. *Sex and the Seasoned Woman.* New York: Random House.

Storr, Anthony. 1988. *Solitude: A Return to the Self.* New York: Ballantine Books.

Summers, Vanessa. 2005. *Buying Solo: The Single Woman's Guide to Buying a First Home.* New York: Perigee.

Thoreau, Henry David. 1990 (originally published in 1854; many publishers). *Walden.* Philadelphia: Courage Books.

Tiger, Lionel. 1992. *The Pursuit of Pleasure.* New York: Little, Brown.

Trimberger, E. Kay. 2005. *The New Single Woman.* Boston: Beacon Press.

Wallerstein, Judith S., and Sandra Blakeslee. 1996. *Second Chances: Men, Women, and Children a Decade after Divorce.* Boston: Houghton Mifflin.

Yount, David. 1997. *Spiritual Simplicity.* New York: Simon & Schuster.

_____. 2005. *Celebrating the Rest of Your Life: A Baby Boomer's Guide to Spirituality.* Minneapolis: Augsburg.

Index

wellness, 107
Wesley, John, 4–5
Wetering, Janwillem van de, 80
Whitman, Walt, 156, 163
widows and widowers, 3, 155–156
Wilde, Oscar, 98, 101, 120
will, 47
Williams, John Alden, 80
Williams, Tennessee, 17
Willis, Bruce, 103
Winslet, Kate, 102
Witness Protection Program, 158
women: health resources, 115; single, stereotypes about, 13, 160; in the workforce, 4

Woods, Tiger, 62
Wouk, Herman, 80
Wurtzel, Elizabeth, 20

A Year in Provence (Mayle), 138
Young Men's Christian Association, 88
young singles, scripts for: living alone, 151–152; living together, 152–153
Young Women's Christian Association, 88

"zero sum" universe, 165

About the Author

DAVID YOUNT is a critically acclaimed author and nationally syndicated columnist for Scripps Howard; his column, "Amazing Grace," has been circulated weekly for over a decade to newspapers with a combined readership of 25 million. His published books include *Growing in Faith: A Guide for the Reluctant Christian*; *Ten Thoughts to Take into Eternity: Living Wisely in Light of the Afterlife*; *Celebrating the Rest of Your Life: A Baby Boomer's Guide to Spirituality*; *America's Spiritual Utopias* (Praeger, 2008), and other titles. He also appears as an analyst for PBS and lectures nationwide. He has contributed pieces to *The Washington Post*, *The New York Times*, and *The Wall Street Journal*.

Books by David Yount

Growing in Faith:
  A Guide for the Reluctant Christian

Breaking through God's Silence:
  A Guide to Effective Prayer

Spiritual Simplicity:
  Simplify Your Life and Refresh Your Spirit

Ten Thoughts to Take into Eternity:
  Living Wisely in Light of the Afterlife

Be Strong and Courageous:
  Letters to My Children about Being Christian

What Are We to Do?:
  Living the Sermon on the Mount

Faith under Fire:
  Religion's Role in the American Dream

The Future of Christian Faith in America

Celebrating the Rest of Your Life:
  A Baby Boomer's Guide to Spirituality

How the Quakers Invented America

Growing in Faith:
  A Guide for the New Millennium

America's Spiritual Utopias:
  The Quest for Heaven on Earth